THE WRECKER'S
TO SOUTH WEST DEVON

BY PETER MITCHELL

PART TWO

LENGTH BETWEEN PERPS   225'- 2"
BREADTH MOULDED   23'- 10½"
DEPTH   13'- 11¾"

Corrected at Sheerness Yard to May 1908
Corrected at Pembroke Dockyard to Jan.ry 1914

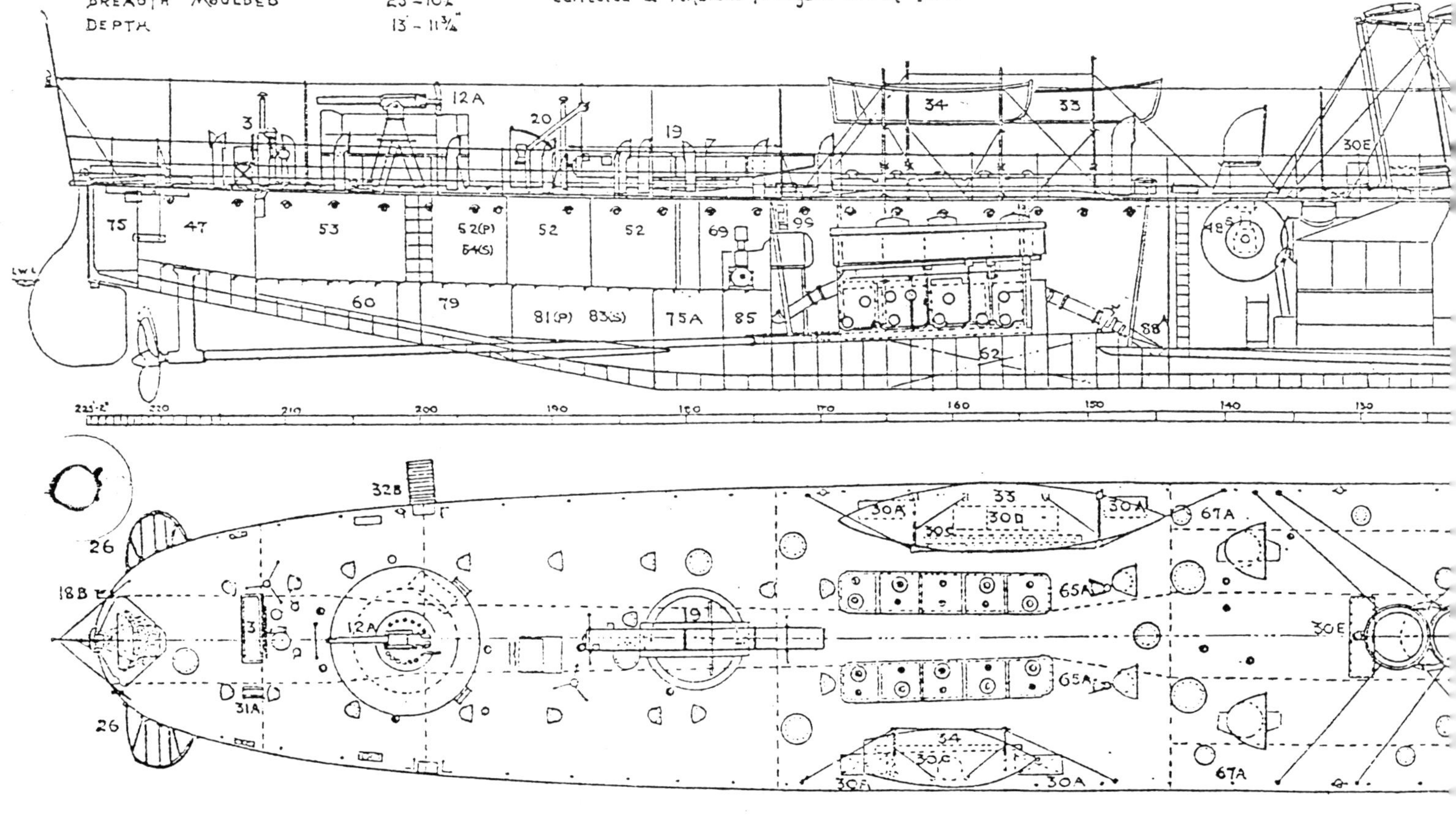

12A
3
20
19
34 33
30E

75 47 53 52(P) 54(S) 52 52 69 99 48

60 79 81(P) 83(S) 75A 85 88

52

225'-2" 220 210 200 190 180 170 160 150 140 130

32B
26
18B
3 12A 19
31A
26

33
30A 30D 30A 67A
30C
65A
30E
65A

34
30B
30A 30A 67A

2

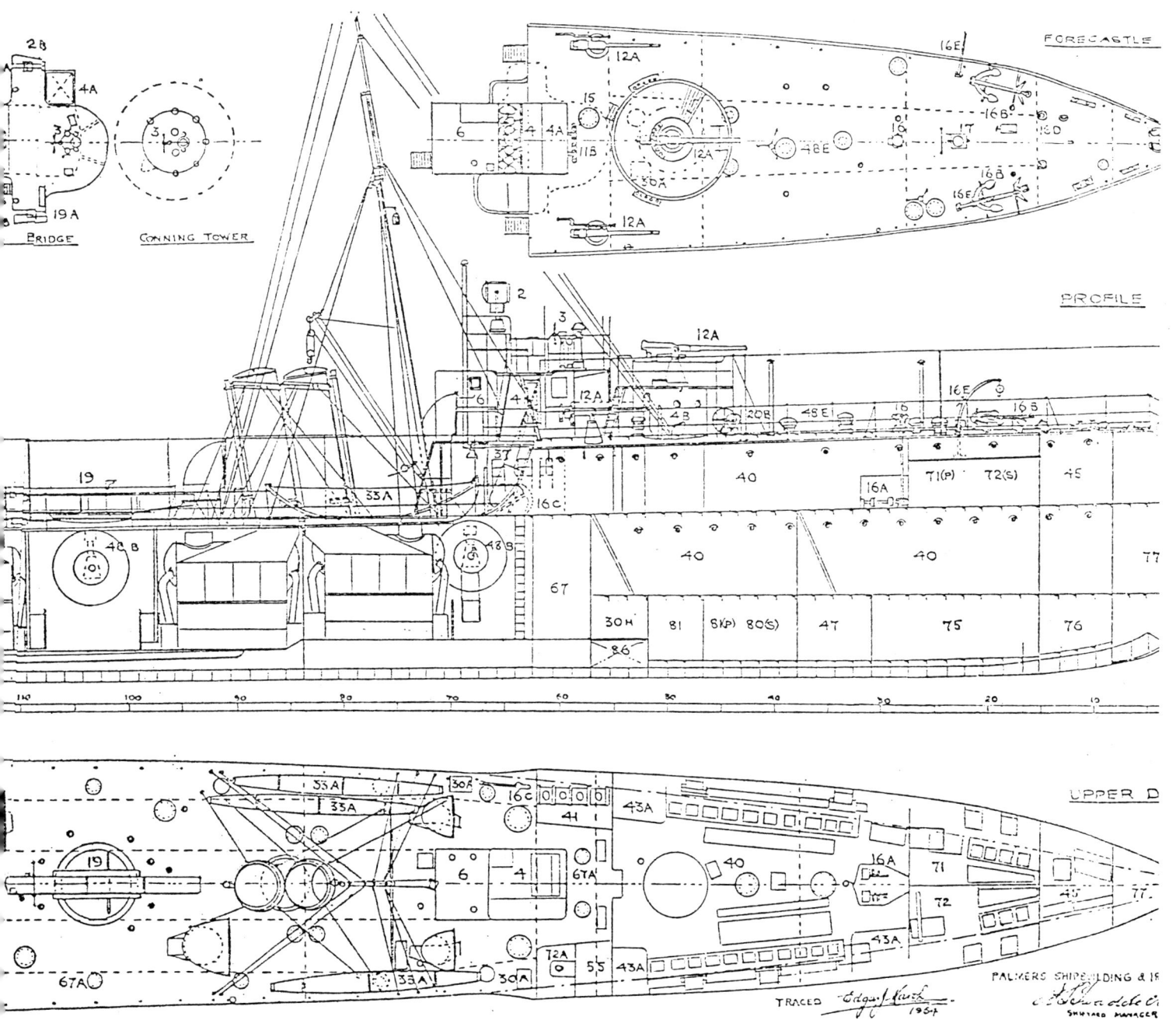

BRIDGE   CONNING TOWER

FORECASTLE

PROFILE

UPPER D

TRACED *Edgar Kirk* 1934

PALMERS SHIPBUILDING & IR

SHIPYARD MANAGER

3

Introduction

When I wrote the Wreckers Guide To South West Devon I had not intended to write a sequel, and so this second volume is not as geographically tidy as it's predecessor. However the elements that made the first volume so popular have remained to the forefront, and I hope that divers find this book as easy to use as the first. For this volume I have extended the depth range to fifty meters but have limited the wrecks to those that, with one exception, can still be found by using marks in the area between Whitsands Bay in Cornwall to Prawle Point in South West Devon, thereby just staying in sight of the book's title. However many of the wrecks are in less than fifty feet and some can even be snorkled on.

As before I have personally dived all the wrecks and the marks are clear and easy to use. Where any difficulties arise photographs help to pinpoint the marks, and once again I reiterate the fact that if I can find these wrecks and then you should have no real difficulty.

Once again I would like to thank all my diving partners for the help they have given me, especially Roger Webber, Malcom Brock and Stever Carpenter who helped me on some of the deeper dives, and 'Brasso' Brassington, Mike 'Asda' Bernard and Dave 'My Flower' Page who just kept turning up to do the dives.

Peter Mitchell, January 1992

4

CONTENTS

Published by
SOUND DIVING
PUBLICATIONS

© Peter Mitchell 1992

CHAPTER 1

AT THE EDGE ... INTRODUCTION

If you look at a chart of the Approaches to Plymouth you will see that once you get below forty metres the wrecks dot the chart like a rash. With position finding electronics in wider circulation, the diver can now attempt to locate wrecks that only a few years ago would have seemed impossible, and with ever more sophisticated equipment the diver can now go deeper and stay longer. However even with all this sophistication the mark one eyeball is still a very valuable tool, and old fashioned marks can still give as good, if not better results, even if the wreck is some considerable distance offshore.

The following wrecks are right at the edge of what you could expect a mark to deliver. But with proper usage, and a good echo sounder to confirm, the marks given here will put you right on the wrecks every time. You might say why bother? Decca after all will probably get you straight there. Well maybe I am old fashioned, but punching buttons on a magic box is all very well, and with proper use it will usually deliver the goods. However sorting out the marks, lining them up, and then trying to drop your anchor right down the funnell is much more satisfying, especially when you get it right.

Going inside the *Medoc*

THE WRECK OF H.M.S. FOYLE

HMS Foyle

Experience with earlier types of destroyers had convinced the Navy that going just for speed was a delusion. What they really needed was a much tougher type of boat that could keep going at relatively high speeds when the weather got really rough. To this end the Navy commissioned a new type of destroyer that was to provide the bench mark for all future Navies, and designated it the River Class. Well over thirty were built before the Great War, and one of them was H.M.S. Foyle.

Laid down at Cammel Lairds shipyard in August 1902, the *Foyle* was launched in February of the following year and entered service thirteen months later in 1904. 225 feet long with a top speed of twenty five and a half knots, the *Foyle* was armed with four twelve pounder guns and two torpedo tubes. At first her slower speed (anything under thirty knots was considered odd) caused some ill-formed comment, but it was soon realised that the sturdyness of her design allowed her to maintain her top speed in all but the worst

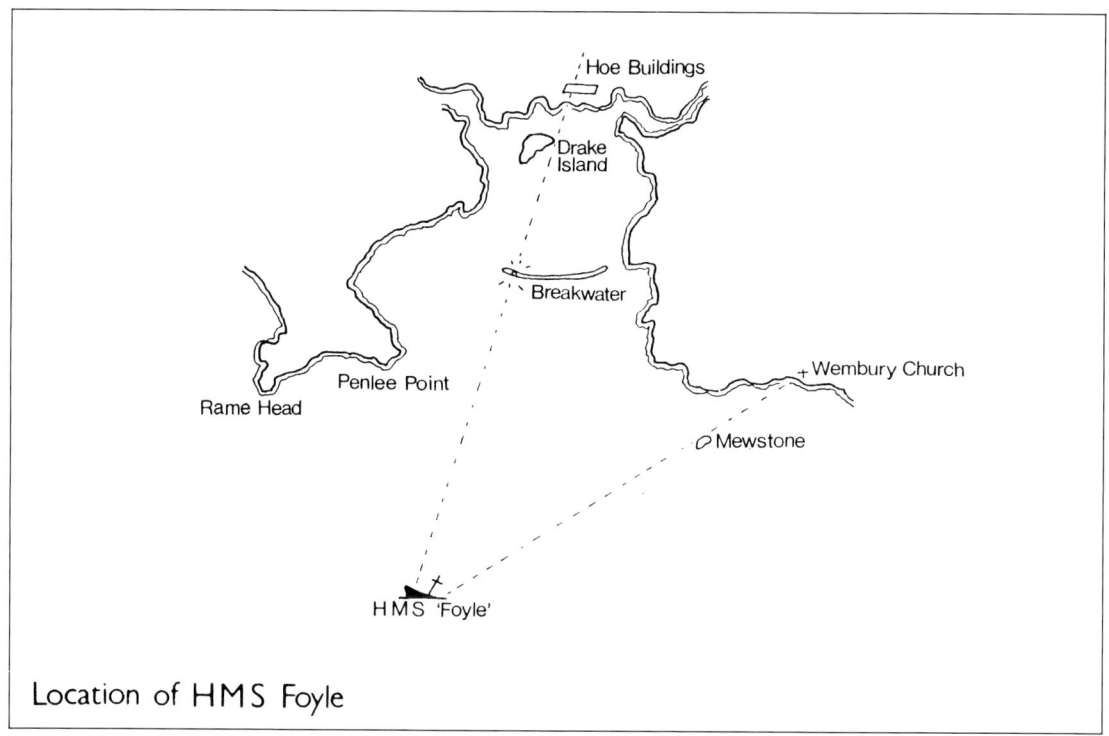

Location of HMS Foyle

conditions, and soon her critics were silenced.

When War broke out the *Foyle* found herself performing patrol and escort duties in the killing ground of the Dover Straights. On the night of March 15 1917 she hit a mine, and the force of the explosion blew away the whole of her bows forward of the bridge, killing twenty seven of her crew of seventy. Unbelievably the stern half stayed afloat, and it was decided to tow this to Plymouth, presumably to graft on another bow. What the thoughts were of the tug crews who had to place the tow on a helpless drifting hulk in the middle of a potential minefield we can only guess, but eventually the tow was established and the *Foyle* was led away towards Plymouth. After surviving the minefields and slipping through a screen of maurauding E boats, the salvage crew on the *Foyle* just could not keep up with the water pouring through her ruptured plates, and only a few miles from Plymouth H.M.S. *Foyle* gave up the fight and sank in fifty metres of water about 4 miles off the Mewstone. One of the main troubles about diving on a wreck as deep as the *Foyle* is the lack of time you can spend on her. If you are diving this wreck on a one-off basis, then you really will not have a clue where you are on it unless you stumble onto the gun at the stern section, or blunder into the bridge. You really need to go with somebody who knows the wreck so that they can explain to you after the dive where you have been, or pray for uncharacteristically good visibility. Having said that, the one thing that anyone will recognise is the brass. On the few dives that I have done on this wreck everywhere that I have looked there seemed to be lumps of non-ferrous metal, either portholes, (too firmly fixed for me) large copper pipes and brass valves, or on one occasion, what seemed to be the top of a binnacle.

The *Foyle* now lies on a sandy seabed with what appears to be a thirty degree list. Most of the portside is buried in the sand and the rest of the hull has caved in. However her boilers seem to be mostly intact, although other divers say that one boiler is probably buried in the wreckage. At the bridge end is a great mound of iron plates and girders covered in shoals of swirling pollack and pouting. Somewhere in all that junk should be three of the *Foyle's* twelve pounder guns, but I must confess I have never seen them. Lobsters abound on the wreck as do congers, and because the wreck is heavily fished by local anglers quite a bit of fishing gear is left lurking to entangle the unwary diver.

Somewhere towards the stern are the remains of the torpedo tubes. Back in the Sixties rumour has it that one of the *Foyle's* torpedo tubes still has a torpedo left in it. When this torpedo was duly liberated and placed on dry land, the salvors became so blinkered as to the profit on the non-ferrous metal, that they seemed to completely forget all about the couple of hundred pounds

Just some of the brass recovered (sadly, not by me)

Mayflower Post House

Grand Hotel

Stone Buttress

Flats

Moathouse Tower

Flats

P L Y M O U T H   H O E

Sealine

Breakwater Lighthouse

Wembury Church

Mewstone

MARK TWO

MARK ONE

Telegraph from the *Foyle*

What the *Medoc* must have looked like

THE HALFWAY WRECK

When France finally fell to the invading Nazi Hordes, most of her still powerful Navy became immobilised in various Ports around the world, awaiting the decision of its government whether to surrender to the Germans or place their vessels at the disposal of the hard-pressed Allies. Meanwhile the French Government was in crisis. Some members fled to England, other decided to co-operate with the Germans and so formed the Vichy government which was roundly condemned by the so-called 'Free French' under a little known General called De Gaulle. Whilst all this was going on, the British under Churchill, decided to take matters in hand and promptly commandeered at gun point the French fleet stationed at Aboukir, an episode that even today, sill rankles. The Allies then went on to commandeer every other French vessel that it could lay its hands on. One of these was the cargo carrier the *Medoc*. 237 feet long, 34 feet wide with a displacement of 1166 tons, the *Medoc* was loaded with ammunition, mostly 3.5 shell cases and cordite when she approached the vicinity of the Eddystone on the afternoon of 26 November 1940. A lookout spotted a plane coming towards the ship but decided it was friendly. He soon realised his mistake when the plane opened fire and raked the *Medoc* with machine gun fire. As the plane turned away into the gloom of late afternoon the crew thought that they were in for a lucky escape. However the enemy aircraft was just getting its act

of Amatol explosive that was by now highly unstable. When the Poice arrived on the scene they found the scrappers gaily hacking at the torpedo with lump hammers and crowbars, with the explosive oozing out of the cracks that they had made. Seems unbelievable doesn't it? But as I say it is only a rumour. The *Foyle* is probably the deepest wreck off Plymouth that you can still find just on the marks. But because she only stands up about fifteen feet from the seabed, and is such a long way down, a good echo sounder is really a necessity. Once you have found her you should have no further trouble. If you can arrange a series of dives on the *Foyle,* so much the better as it is frustrating to see something you cannot get off in the short time available. In recent years local clubs have had some very impressive trophies from this wreck, but for the dedicated wrecker there is still an awful lot left.

together. This time as it flew towards the *Medoc* it rattled off a couple of bursts with its machine guns and then dropped a torpedo with devastating effect. The *Medoc* sank like a stone. So quickly did she go that all thirty-nine of her crew perished with her.

Today the *Medoc* lies way down, 150 feet to the bottom. She is still more or less upright and situated in position 50 15 06 north 04 14 10 west. This position is exact and if you are using Decca then you will be right on the wreck. If you are using marks then I am afraid that you will have a problem. In the introduction to this chapter

I said that you could just find this wreck on marks. Well you could when I wrote that, but unfortunately the two very large chimneys on the Cattewater power station, which formed the principle mark, were demolished in late 1990. Without these chimneys it is almost impossible to recognise other marks clearly enough. However for those who want to try, I have drawn out the old marks. There are three marks in all, and two are quite easy to find. But without the chimney mark it is very difficult to 'fine tune' accurately enough to put your anchor right on it. Still they will put you in the 'ball park' and

11

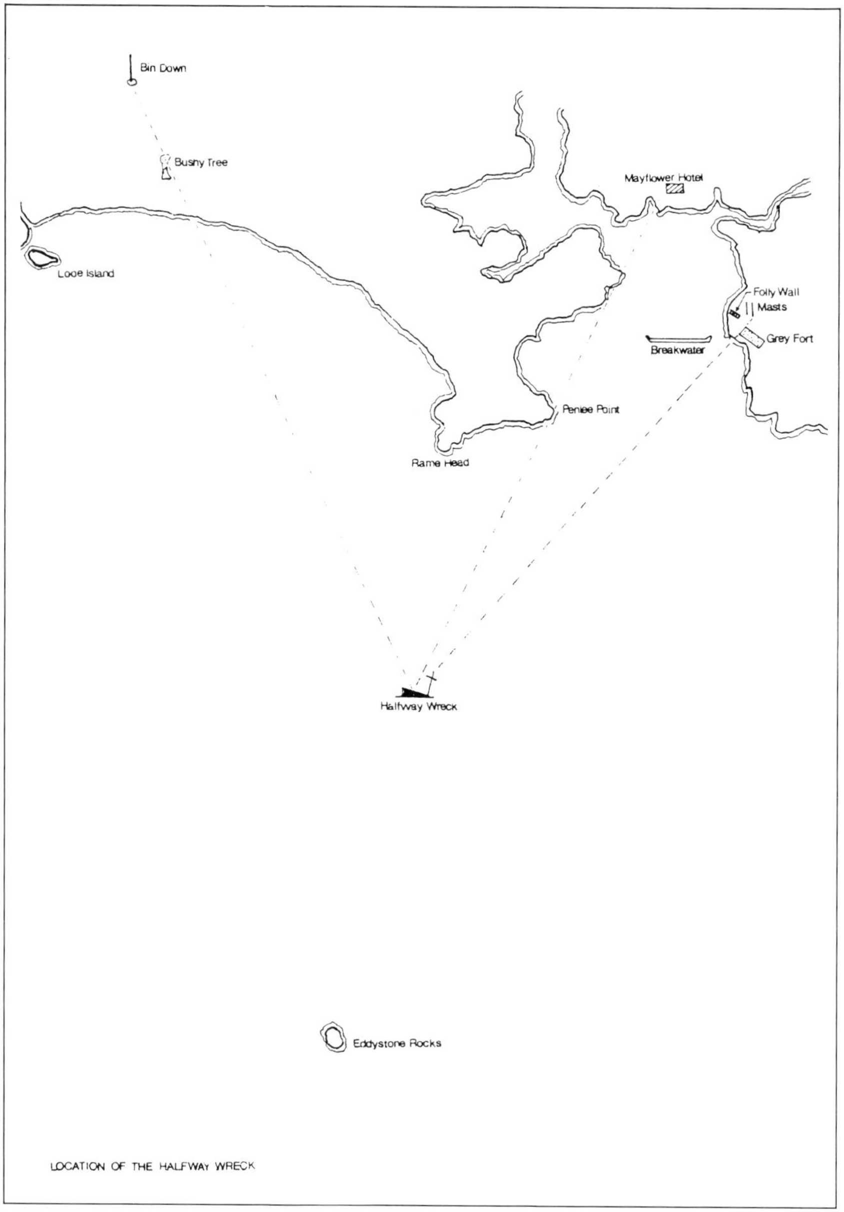

then your little black box can take over. Make no mistake, the wreck is well worth the effort. Local dive skipper Roger Webber in his promotional blurb describes this wreck as 'dripping with portholes' and he is absolutely right. On my one and only dive on the *Medoc* I counted five portholes and I was only in the middle.

As I said earlier, the *Medoc* lies more or less upright and does not show all that many scars of battle. She has a small bridge situated towards the rear that you can swim in and out of and look at the hole where the compass binnacle was

Map labels:
Bin Down
Busny Tree
Looe Island
Mayflower Hotel
Folly Wall
Masts
Breakwater
Grey Fort
Penlee Point
Rame Head
Halfway Wreck
Eddystone Rocks

LOCATION OF THE HALFWAY WRECK

Decompressing on the
Halfway Wreck

discovered. This was a significant find because up until about 1984 nobody really knew what the identity of the Halfway wreck really was. The ring around the binnacle had the makers name on it, and from this a positive identification was made. If you swim towards the bows you will come across one of the holds that is chock full of shell cases. These are all empty and so make good souvenirs. (Make sure you remove the peccussion caps at the bottom.) They are however quite heavy and more than one diver has had to jettisson his shellcase during the long assent. By far the best way is to tie them on the line and so do your decompression in comfort. The Halfway wreck is a favourite with the charter boat fishing skippers and as such is festooned with fishing tackle. It is difficult to see the fine line and the hooks seem to snag you all the time. Although the wreck is relatively small, it gives the impression of a much larger wreck, probably because of its depth and so it is difficult to find out just where you are on it. However although the Medoc is deep the visibility is usually quite good, about twenty feet, so you might not know where you are on her but at least you can see what you are doing. And there is plenty to see. Although the steam whistle, binnacle and telegraph have long gone, the bridge is still largely intact, the holds are still full of shell cases, and portholes seem to be all around. This is all largely due to the fact that the Medoc is a deep and difficult wreck to find and so not that many divers venture out to her, and of course those that do just cannot spend enough time on her unless they get organised.

So there the Medoc lies. A deep wreck, hard to find and so largely untouched. Definately not one for the casual plunger. But if you are the serious sort of wrecker and you can get your team organised, then I think you will find the Halfway wreck very interesting indeed.

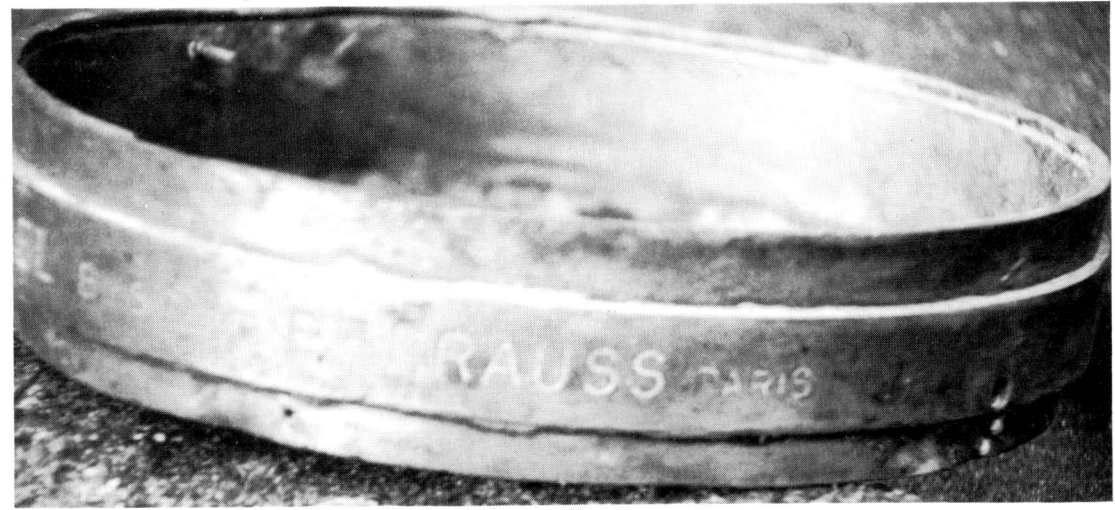

Big Malcolm with the Medoc's steam whistle

The compass ring that identified the Medoc

THE WRECK OF THE SAILING BARQUE OREGON

Just before the turn of the century, in spite of all the advances made by steamships, sailing vessels of all shapes and sizes still carried the bulk of Britain's trade. Whilst fast clipper ships like the *Herzogin Cecilie* were undoubtably the glamour boys, sailing barques like the *Oregon* were the ships that made up the backbone of England's merchant marine, and carried cargo's all over the world, often in appauling weather. Today we think that deadlines and clockwatching are modern diseases, but even in those days cargo's had to be delivered on time or Captains were likely to be sacked on the spot, especially if the owners lost money. The pressures on the Captain were immense, especially if he had share in the cargo. With navigation still a chancy business in confined areas like the English Channel, mistakes were bound to happen and if cast on a lee shore like South Devon's these mistakes usually proved fatal. On December 18 1890 the *Oregon*, a steel hulled threemasted sailing barque of 810 tonnes, was in the last stages of her voyage from Iquique in Chile to her home port of Newcastle loaded with a cargo of nitrate of soda. As she came up the Channel towards Falmouth the weather deteriorated with fierce squalls of rain lashing the ship, and her skipper, Captain Lowe, decided to put into Falmouth to pick up a Pilot. He left later that evening and raced up towards Plymouth in the freezing gale force winds and tumultous seas, with the night seemingly getting darker and darker. With visibility cut down by the now torrential rain, the *Oregon* weathered Rame Head and set course for Bolt Head. Now if you have ever been on this bit of ocean you will know that it is very easy to actually steer for Bolt Tail instead of Bolt Head, a course that will bring you into the last bit of Bigbury Bay. Why Captain Lowe and the Pilot made this mistake we shall never know, although in the weather conditions that they encountered it would have been easy enough. What we do know is late that night the *Oregon* struck the Book Rocks just off Thurleston Beach. Captain Lowe immediately

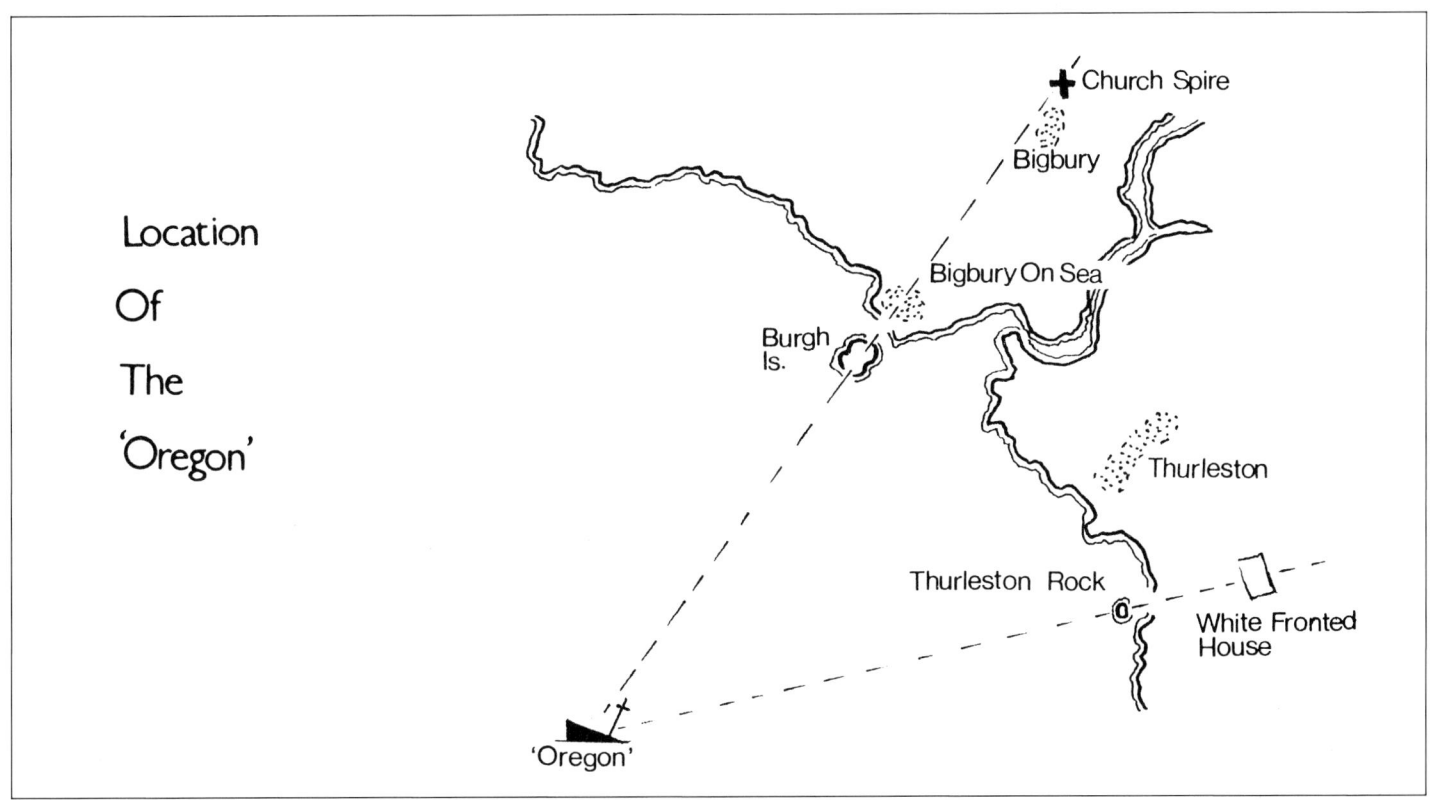

Location Of The 'Oregon'

Church Spire

Bigbury

Bigbury On Sea

Burgh Is.

Thurleston

Thurleston Rock

White Fronted House

'Oregon'

ordered the ship about and managed to claw off the rocks before becoming impaled on the sharp granite reef. Alas his prompt action was to no avail, as the Oregon was badly holed and taking water in very vast. Realising that he would have to abandon the vessel, Captain Lowe ordered the lifeboats lowered. The first boat was swamped by the huge seas and immediately sank, but the other boat was successfully launched and Captain Lowe and all his crew managed to scramble into it without losing anybody in the process. For twelve hours they floated on the stormy sea in complete darkness. With the wind blowing and the huge sea's crashing down ontot he boat it must have been a nightmare. At last one of the crew spotted a light on the shore. It was a local labourer who had heard the barque striking, and with his lamp he guided the Oregon's lifeboat safely to the little fishing village of Hope where the inhabitants took in the by now nearly dead crewmen and made them comfortable in their own homes. Meanwhile the Oregon, swamped by the mountainous seas, sank soon after her crew left. For her there was to be no save haven at Hope Cove.

Nowadays the remains of the Oregon lie in 110 feet of water on a flat sandy bottom, and are extremely difficult to find. The marks are easy to locate, but allow a certain parralax error, which means that once on the marks you will have to switch on your echo sounder and use that to pinpoint the wreck. It is not easy, but if you are successful the dive is certainly worthwhile providing the visibility is reasonable. The wreck lies as she sank with the bows the most prominent and intact feature, with a large anchor

Far left: The Cutty Sark — very similar to the Oregon

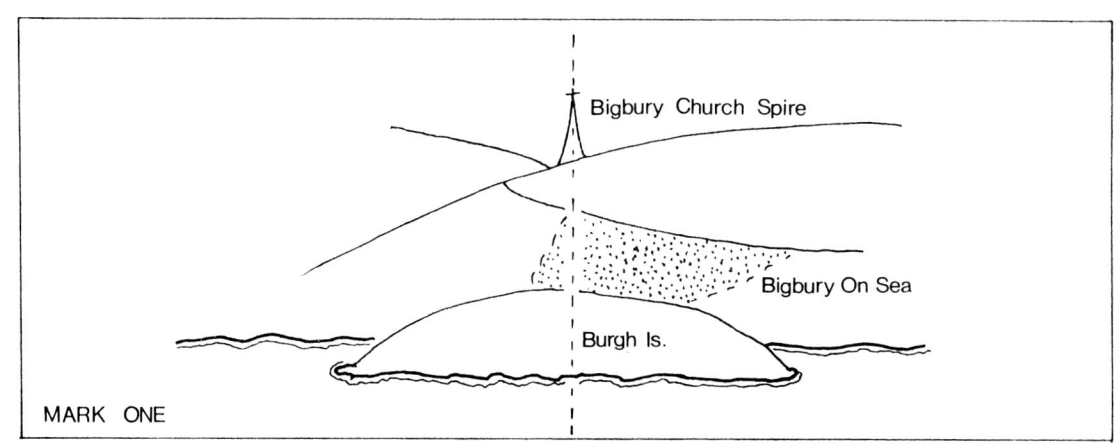

MARK ONE

Bigbury Church Spire

Bigbury On Sea

Burgh Is.

Shown with Thurlestone Rock to the left to give better contrast in the photo.

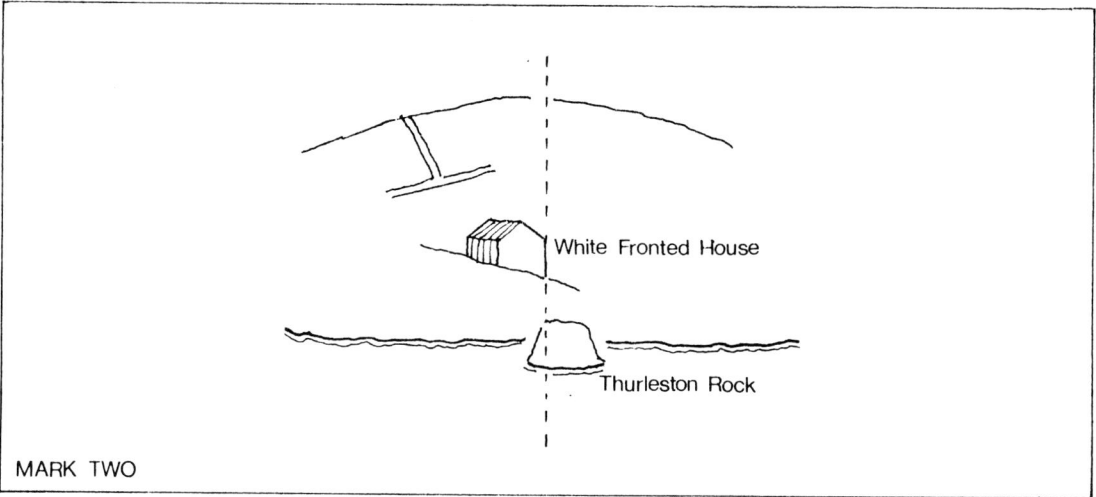

White Fronted House

Thurleston Rock

MARK TWO

16

lying nearby in the sand. The *Oregon's* sides have collapsed leaving the inside of the hull exposed with all her ribs and keel posts showing, and across her lies one of her masts. She is a very compact wreck and easy to get around in the limited time. Underneath the rusting iron plates of her hull live quite a number of lobsters who obviously do not see a lot of divers, and small congers also become quite inquisitive when you peer underneath the some of the hull plates. Pollock and pouting shoal about this wreck in some numbers, and on the bows some very nice plumrose anemones are attached. Because the wreck is so compact you can hover above it and get to see nearly all the wreck spread out before you, and that is a sight that is worth waiting for.

If you have dived on other sailing vessels like the Hertzogin Cecilie, you will get some idea of their relative sizes, and realise how lucky the crew were to get off before she sank. On this wreck however, visibility is all. If the visibility is bad then you will just not appreciate what a pretty little wreck this is, so it is well worth picking your time, preferably a flat calm sunny day, near slack water, and no rain for a few days. (The mouth of the River Avon drops tons of silt over the area after heavy rain.) Winter is a very good time if you can crack the cold, as the water gets that wonderful ice blue quality and fifty foot visibility is a real possibility. By the way, do not be misled by reports that the *Oregon* is just a few rusting iron plates. The people who say this usually cannot find the wreck. Go and see for yourself.

Oregon,
looking through
the stern section

Chapter 2

Whitsands Bay Wrecks ...

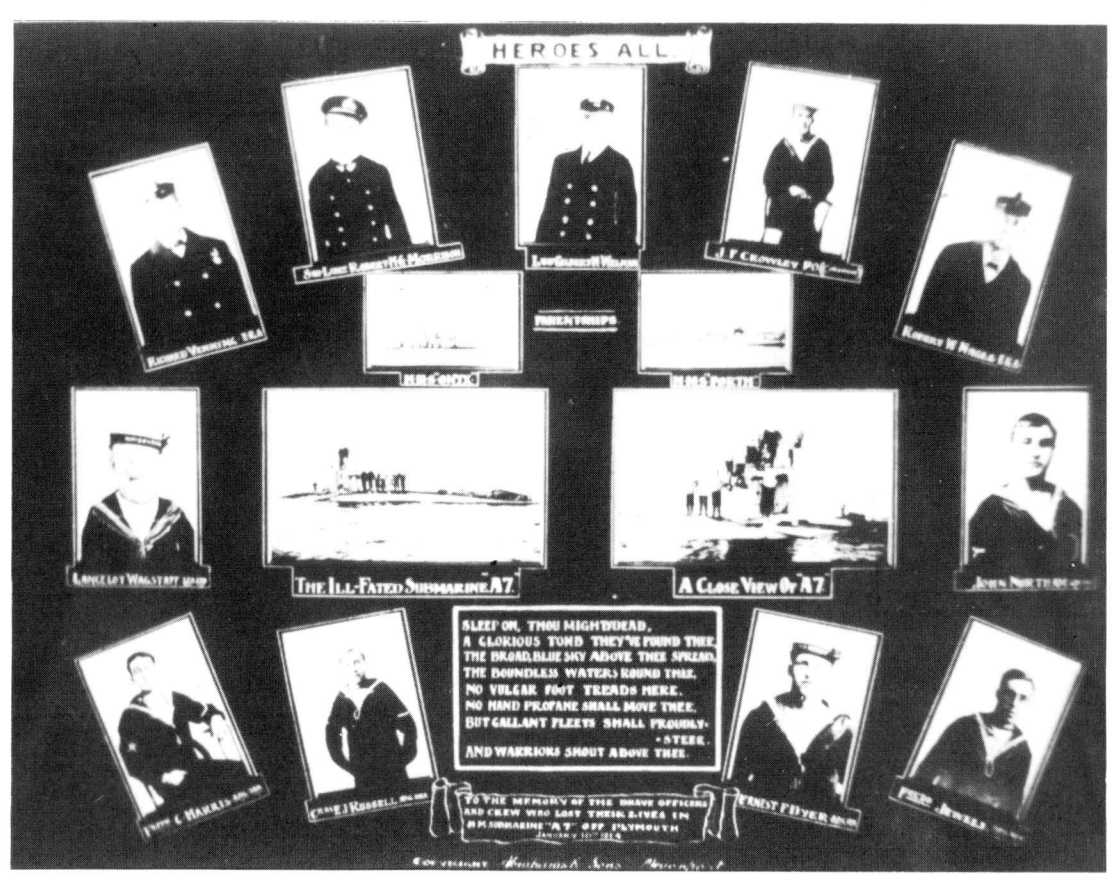

Memorial postcard and photograph struck in honour of the crew of the A7

Introduction

Whitsands Bay with its broad sweep and wide sandy beaches was a welcome sight for many a seasick passenger, because it meant that the safe haven of Plymouth was finally at hand. With a small sixteenth century chapel resting like a pimple on its towering cliffs, Rame Head was easy to identify and gave most vessels a good landmark. Even so many ships came to grief in this area especially fishing boats working out of Looe, Portwrinkle and Plymouth.

On January 17 1934 the steam trawler *Chancellor*, fog bound and steaming into the teeth of a south westerly gale, hit the rocks at the bottom of the cliffs around Portwrinkle. In the mountainous seas the Plymouth lifeboat could not get near, and in the end a breeches buoy was rigged which plucked the crew to safety before the *Chancellor* was smashed to pieces and

scattered on the shore. In 1976 the *Emma Christ*, and ex Naval M.F.V. was swept onto the rocks at the base of Tregantle cliffs. Two of the crew managed to get off the strickened vessel but the others had to be rescued by helicopter.

We all know about the most famous of all the Whitsands Bay wrecks, the *James Egan Layne*, (see Book One) but not so many divers visit the wreck of the armed merchant cruiser *Rosehill*, because it is difficult to find and quite a long ride in an inflatable. However it is worth the effort. The last wreck is that of the submarine A7. Because it is a War Grave I have given no marks for it. However the best Dive Skippers in Plymouth know its location and are happy to take responsible divers out to her. But please remember the rules. Look but do not touch.

The *Rosehill*, formerly the *Minster*

THE WRECK OF THE ROSEHILL

Two miles out from Portwrinkle lies one of the hardest wrecks to locate along this part of the coast. She is the armed merchant ship *Rosehill.*

Built in 1911 by S. P. Austin and Son of Sunderland, she was first launched as the *Minster* by her owners Stephen Clarke and Company. 314 feet long with a gross tonnage of 2788 tons, the *Minster* was fitted with a triple expansion engine made by the Sunderland firm of North East Marine Engineering. In 1914 she was sold to a Welsh Steamship Company called W. J. Tillet and was renamed the *Rosehill.* At the outbreak of the First World War she was requisitioned by the Admiralty as a collier and armed with a small gun, probably a four pounder.

During September 1917 the *Rosehill* was enroute from Cardiff to Devonport when the Geman submarine U 40 torpedoed her and she sank in about 100 feet of water at the edge of a reef, surrounded by large outcrops of rock. This fact conspires to fool many a person with an echo sounder, and the only effective way to find her is to use the marks, which will put you right on the boilers. However the marks can be almost elusive and I will come back to them in a moment.

Because the *Rosehill* lies so far along the coast from Plymouth, and because of its difficult marks, the *Rosehill* is not extensively dived. Often the visibility is not much more than ten feet, and sometimes a lot less, so most of the charter skippers prefer the *Egan Layne* because it is nearer and has much better visibility. Whilst the marks are easy enough to spot on the land, the telegraph poles in the first mark tend to vanish on a clear sunny day. Even binoculars cannot bring them back, but sometimes a good set of polaroid sunglasses can. So ideally you want a calm clear day with a touch of cloud.

The first mark is the one to use for the main approach, and the 'stopper' is the second mark.

Now this mark is a real pain because you have to adjust its position for the state of the tide (yes really). It took me two years to realise this, because we had dived it before at the low range of the tide. No special reason, just coincidence, but the marks always worked perfectly. One day we went out to the wreck on a spring high and I just could not find it. After nearly two hours of looking the crew were about ready to lynch me, when a local fisherman came up and told me that his buoy (a fairy liquid bottle) was right on it. It looked right out to me but by now I was desperate. A diver went down to check it out, and there she was, correctly positioned on the first mark but much further along the 'stopper' mark. I have never come across this sort of mark before, and I can't say I care very much for it, but I have tried all sorts of other marks and they just do not work, so I guess I am stuck with it.

Still after all the hassle the *Rosehill* is well worth it. This was the first wreck I ever dived with a gun on it, and that is only one of it's many attractions. The ship is lying almost upside down

Some brass valves from the *Rosehill*

20

in parts and it takes some time to get your bearings, especially as the visibility is usually not very good. Still there is plenty of brass on this wreck, but you will need to come well prepared for most of it is well bolted on. On my first dive on the *Rosehill* there was no entrance into her engine room except for a small crack in the hull. Over the years however, this crack has turned into quite a gaping hole, and although not quite big enough to get into properly, you can certainly see enough to hope that the hole gets a lot wider. Around the boiler is a huge jumble of metal, parts of the hull and pieces of the deck all lumped onto one another. In amongst all this are some brass valves bolted to the plating, and some fairly large bearing blocks. At the bows is an anchor and chain and part of a mast complete with the pullies that must have helped support the derricks that loaded and unloaded the ship.

Somewhere amongst all this is the gun. I must confess that I never can quite put my finger straight on this, and usually have to be led to it by one of my partners. Still I do like looking at it, even though I am not too sure what type it is. Nice big barrel, elevating and training wheels, mounting with calibration ring, the lot almost ready to fire. Great.

Besides the brass and the gun, there are an awful lot of fish as well. Pouting and Pollack you would expect, and they are here in huge numbers. The exception are Bass. I was surprised to see them here on one dive maybe they were only visiting. A few years ago there were sensational stories in the press about a giant conger eel attacking divers thighs, (I always wondered about that) and although there are congers on the wreck, I can't say that I noticed any of them attacking divers. But then, as I have already said, the visibility is not that good.

Once you have dived the *Rosehill* a few times you begin to make some order out of the jumble, and you begin to notice that things are missing, and that is what makes this wreck really interesting. For instance, where is the bridge? Is it underneath the upturned part of the hull, or has it been torn off and is now lying some way away from the wreck? If I find out be sure I will let you know. Better still, you find it and let me know.

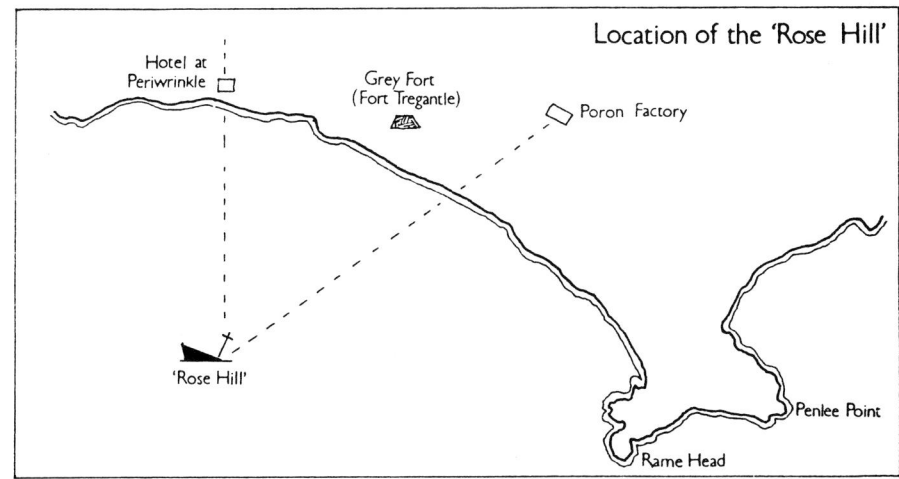

Location of the 'Rose Hill'

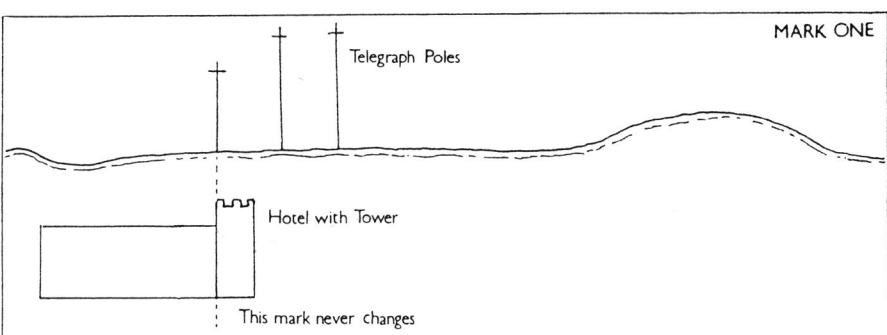

MARK ONE

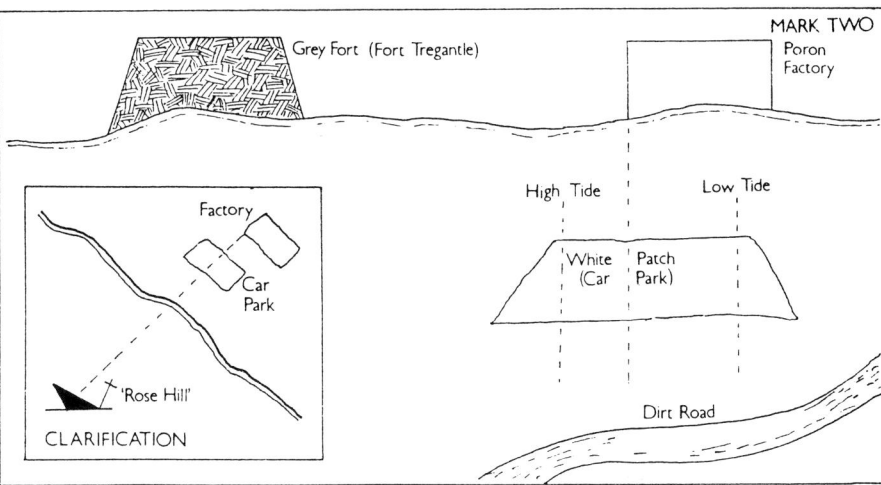

MARK TWO

THE WRECK OF THE SUBMARINE A7

Divers put a flag on the periscope of the A7 to mark the anniversary of her loss

A stern view of the A7

All the A boats shown here were sunk at least once

Developed from the basic *Holland* design, the A class of submarine was the Royal Navy's first attempt at an all British submarine. Among its innovations was a proper conning tower which prevented the submarine being swamped when running on the surface. Additional torpedo tubes were also added, and the whole boat lengthened by about forty feet, which made it more stable and seaworthy. Unfortunately, these new submarines retained the *Holland's* worst defect, which was a pitifully small reserve of buoyancy. Although still largely experimental, the A boats wre relatively successful, and some even saw active service in 1914 if only in a training role. However survival became of crucial importance for the crews of these submarines, because at one time or another every single one of them sank at least once, usually with fatal consequences. The *A1*, rammed by the *Berwick Castle*, sank with all hands off the Nab, near the Isle of Wight, in March 1904, and although she was raised a month later she was never recommissioned but sunk later as a target. The *A2* was wrecked whilst on the for sale list, and the *A3* was rammed and sunk by the aptly named *Hazard* in February 1912 with the loss of all hands. The submarine *A4* perished during a collision in Porstmouth Harbour in 1905 when she sank like a stone and drowned all her crew, and on the 8 June 1905 the *A8* suffered an explosion whilst running on the surface and sank just off the Knapp Buoy a few hundred yards from Plymouth's Breakwater. The *A8* was successfully salvaged and after undergoing a complete overhaul she served all through the Great War and ended her days being sold for scrap. Ironically the *A7* had been her escort on that fateful day, and nine years later, in January 1914 the *A7* was once again in the same area, exercising in Whitsands Bay. This time she was engaged in carrying out dummy torpedo attacks on *H.M.S. Pygmy* in company with a flotilla of six other submarines. On the morning of January 16, the flotilla assumed their attack positions and were ordered to dive to a predetermined depth and then resurface. It soon became apparent that the *A7* was in difficulties, when a large stream of bubbles appeared on the surface over the area

THE NAVY'S LAST TRIBUTE
THE FUNERAL SERVICE OVER THE INVISIBLE GRAVE OF THE OFFICERS & CREW OF THE ILL-FATED SUBMARINE "A7" IN WHITSANDBAY MARCH ... 1914 FIRING THE LAST VOLLEY

Funeral service held over the spot where the A7 sank

where she had submerged. All the other submarines returned to the surface safely, but for the A7 disaster had finally struck. The flotilla Commander on board *H.M.S. Pygmy* sped towards the scene and ordered tugs and salvage lighters despatched from Devonport with all possible speed. For some reason however, nobody bothered putting a marker buoy down, so when the tugs arrived with sweeping gear they could not locate the stricken submarine. In the end the Navy spent five days continuosly dragging the sea bed before they found the A7. By the time the divers were ready to go down to the submarine, everybody knew that it was a futile gesture. The A7's crew had all perished. The news of yet another submarine disaster shocked the people of Plymouth and they set up a public fund for the widows and orphans of the

unfortunate crew. The Navy was roundly condemned on all sides for its incompetence, and suffered huge embarrasment at the hands of the National Press who made sarcastic remarks about the inability of the Navy to salvage their own submarines. Meanwhile in Whitsands Bay, the struggle to lift the A7 from the clutches of a muddy sea bed continued. Wires had been passed underneath the submarine and fixed to salvage lighters on the surface. Using winches and the strength of the sea itself in a tidal lift had so far failed to make any impression. The vessel remained firmly lodged in the mud. In the end the Navy, by now in danger of being buried by the abuse hurled at it by a vitriolic press, decided to leave well alone and contented themselves by holding a memorial service over the wrecksite, with a Royal Marine guard firing a salute, and wreaths being tossed upon the calm, silent waters. Thus the A7 became a fitting tomb for all her officers and crew and today, seventy six years later, that is how she still remains.

Of all the wrecks that I have dived on this has to be the most poignant. The phrase a war grave conjures up neat rows of white crosses, somewhere in a foreign field half forgotten. The A7 is much, much more immediate than that. As you fin down the rope 135 feet to the bottom of Whitsands Bay, the A7 suddenly and completely presents itself, almost as if she is still sailing towards a new destination. To all intents she is still completely intact, lying upright in the mud, down to what would be her surface marks. Her periscope is up, and her conning tower and nearly all her fittings are still in place. She is instantly recognisable from her photographs, and as you hover above her to stop the mud swirling up and obsuring her, you can on a good day see the whole length of the A7 laid out pointing into the Bay, as if sailing quietly on to oblivion. Locked inside forever are her Captain and crew. May their souls rest eternally in peace.

The ill-fated A7 and her crew

CHAPTER 3

FLYING BOATS –
THE AUSTRALIAN CONNECTION

26

If you look across the Cattewater from the Barbican you can see the huge hangars of *R.A.F. Mountbatten*. Now used only for the occasional survival course, *R.A.F. Mountbatten* is virtually deserted, its task completed and the past bravery and sacrifice of its various aircrews now just fading memories. But during the Second World War, Mountbatten was home to *No. 10 Squadron Royal Australian Airforce*, and those now deserted hangars hummed with activity as they serviced the needs of the Squadron's aircraft, *Sunderland* flying boats.

Named after Admiral Batten a Civil War governor of the 'headland and tower', the history of Mountbatten goes back to the Great War when in 1917 *R.N.A.S. Cattewater Seaplane Station* was opened as part of a comprehensive chain of South West bases, who's main task was to bomb U. boats in the Western Approaches. After the Great War ended most of the South Western chain of bases were disbanded, but R.N.A.S Cattewater stayed in operation if only as a storage and cadre unit. However as the decade wore on a modest expansion in the role of the seaplane saw Mountbatten return to full operation, and on October 1 1928 Cattewater Station was renamed Mountbatten and that is the way things have stayed up till the present day.

During the early thirties life at Mountbatten was pleasant and peaceful. Training flights and the odd cruise to the Continent or the Mediterranean relieved the boredom. However as the war in Europe became increasingly apparent 204 Squadron were re-equipped with Mountbatten's first *Sunderlands* in June 1939, and soon became responsible for patrolling the Western Approaches where if hostilities broke out they would once more hunt down the U. boats in one of their favourite killing grounds. When War was finally declared, 204 Squadron had six Sunderlands fully operational, and on 4 September they launched their first operational anti-submarine patrol into a grey Plymouth dawn. After nine hours of uneventful patrolling the crew brought the Sunderland safely back only to be shot at by the local anti-aircraft battery who were thankfully long on determination but short on eyesight.

10 Squadron motto

On 1 April 1940, 204 Squadron moved to Sullom Voe in the Shetlands and the Australians moved in in the shape of *10 Squadron Royal Australian Airforce*. They were to stay for the rest of the war hunting submarines with a brief departure to Wales during the height of the Plymouth Blitz. This made life impossible for the Sunderland crews, who with Plymouth Sound so jammed with shipping could hardly take off without hitting either wandering merchant ships or Naval craft rushing around the Sound trying to avoid being straffed by enemy planes. As the war ended many of the Squadron's Australian personnel were repatriated, and on 5 November 1945 10 Squadron left for good and Mountbatten was transferred from Coastal Command to Maintenance Command. It was the end of its days as a flying boat station.

RAAF PAIR REUNITED

Wynton Thorpe (left) and Jack Horgan with the propeller from the Sunderland flying boat.

By HUGH SCHMITT

Memories of air tragedy

THE captain and flight engineer of a RAAF Sunderland flying boat that crashed into England's Plymouth Sound in heavy fog nearly 45 years ago met in Perth yesterday – the first time they had seen each other since the crash.

They were also reunited with wrecked parts of the aircraft that had lain on the seabed till 1985.

The captain, former Flight-Lieut Wynton Thorpe, of South Australia, and the flight engineer, former Sgt Grattan (Jack) Horgan, of Albany, told graphic stories of that "Black Friday" November night in 1942 when their aircraft crashed, flipped on its back and split.

Five British servicemen, including a Victoria Cross-winner, were killed.

"That flight from Gibraltar to Plymouth on Friday the 13th was a weirdo from the start," said Mr Thorpe.

"We got a meteorological report that forecast calm conditions and we ran into 35-40 knot headwinds with lightning, hail and sleet.

"After we'd reached the point of no return we ran into the thickest fog I'd ever seen and the night itself was as black as the inside of a cat," he said.

With less than 15 minutes of fuel left, Mr Thorpe managed to fly the aircraft to within a few kilometres of the Plymouth breakwater.

Because of the conditions Mr Thorpe was using his altimeter to bring the aircraft down.

"The altimeter was reading 600ft (200m) when we slammed into the sea," he said.

"The first thing I remembered after impact was being in the icy sea."

Mr Thorpe saw a badly-injured passenger, a Royal Navy captain, in the water and towed him towards where he thought the Plymouth breakwater would be.

After 90 minutes in the sea, an RAAF pinnace arrived but the captain was dead.

Mr Thorpe discovered later that the captain was on his way to London to receive a Victoria Cross.

Mr Horgan was standing at his fitter's bench when the Sunderland crashed.

"The aircraft split in half just behind me and I was in the sea," he said.

All of the aircraft's 11-man crew survived, some with serious injuries.

At 23, Mr Thorpe was the youngest member of the crew. At 43, Mr Horgan was the oldest.

In 1985, a group of underwater explorers retrieved the Sunderland's port propeller and reduction gear.

They have been put on display with pictures featuring the all-Australian 10 Squadron at the RAAF Association's museum at Bullcreek.

At 3.30pm tomorrow a memorial plaque alongside the relics will be unveiled by the Minister for Defence, Mr Beazley.

And the two survivors, with their vivid memories of that fateful night, will be in attendance.

Besides hunting U. boats and patrolling the Western Approaches the Sunderlands were also used for transporting personnel to bases as far away as Gibraltar. It was on such a mission that disaster struck for the flying boat captained by Flight Lieutenant Wynton Thorpe. The flight from Gibraltar to Plymouth during November 1942 got off to a bad start right from the beginning. For one thing it was Friday 13, and for another the meteorologists managed to get the weather completely wrong. As Wynton Thorpe, his eleven man crew and five passengers left Gibraltar the forecast was for calm conditions. Almost at once they ran into forty knot headwinds, with lightning and hail thrown in for good measure. As the flying boat bucked and swooped its way towards England the weather increased in ferocity, but by then the boat was at the point of no return. All Wynton Thorpe and his crew could do now was to tough it out. At last the weather changed. No more hail and sleet, just thick, black fog. Thorpe later said that "it was the thickest fog he had ever seen" and "that the night was as black as the inside of a cat". With great skill Wynton Thorpe managed to fly the aircraft to within a few miles of the Plymouth Breakwater, but the fog was so bad he was unsure of where he was or how high he might be above the sea. With less than fifteen minutes of fuel left he decided to try for a landing. Because the conditions were so bad he had to rely completely on his altimeter to bring the seaplane down. He was completely blind. When the altimeter was still reading 600 feet the Sunderland slammed into the water. The shock of the impact devastated the aircraft and split it right in half throwing Thorpe straight into the sea. Almost at once he saw one of the passengers, a Naval Captain, lying in the water and started to tow him to where he thought the Breakwater was. They remained in the sea for over ninety minutes before a rescue pinnance finally found them. Alas the bravery and determination of Wynton Thorpe was to no avail. The Naval Captain was dead and Thorpe near collapse. In the end all eleven crew were saved although most sustained serious injuries. None of the five passengers survived. Later, after he had recovered, Wynton Thorpe was to wonder at the irony of his lucky escape. The Naval Captain that he had tried so hard to rescue had only been on board so that he could come to London to receive the highest award of all, the Victoria Cross. What a terrible price to pay for the Nation's gratitude.

Today all this would just be a fading memory but for a diver called Neil Griffin. He and his mates used to dive around the Breakwater quite a bit and one day they were diving on the inside area between the Breakwater Fort and the Lighthouse when Neil found a large piece of aluminium framing. Now the bottom here is very silty mud, and by the time he had completed his investigation of the metal frame he had stirred up the silt so much that he could not see a thing and so decided to call it a day and surfaced. Unfortunately the boat was drifting, and by the

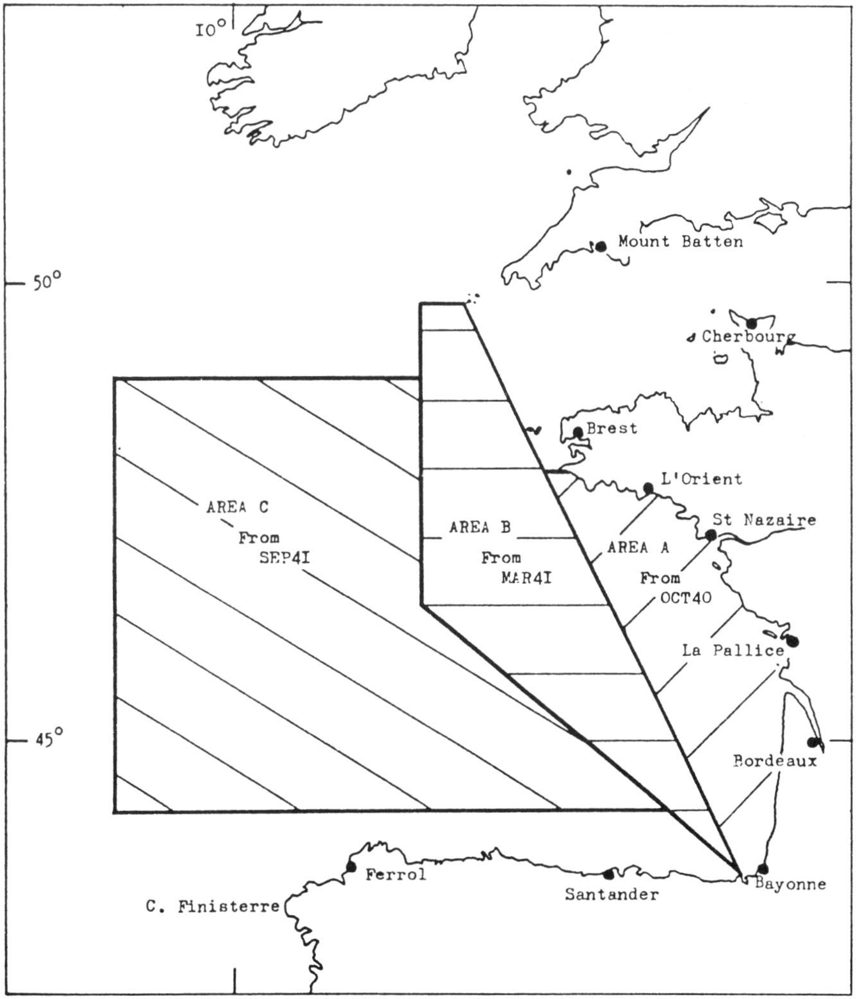

time he got picked up and was back on board he really had very little idea of where he had actually been diving. Still Neil is nothing if not determined, and over the next few months he searched and searched (talk about positive thinking) and finally found the remains of what he thought were two Sunderlands. One was really mangled and spread over quite a large area, but the other was recognisable as two bits of one plane. Over several dives Neil explored this

Above: 10 Squadron patrol area

Left: The propellor dismantled and cleaned

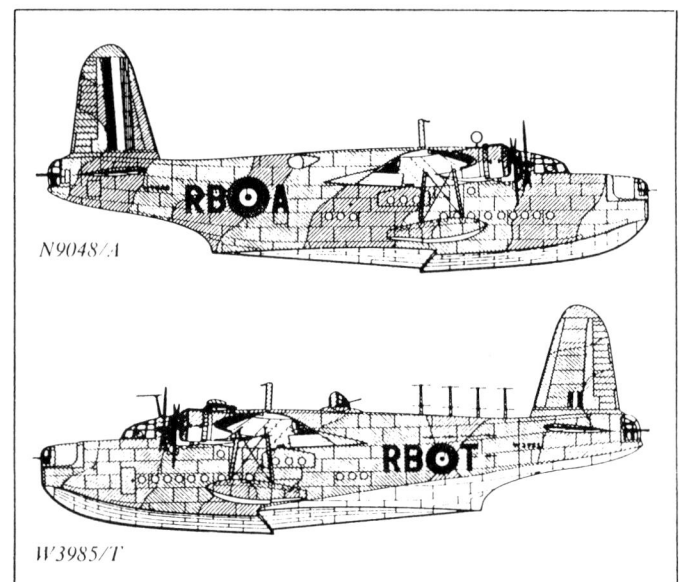

N9048/A

W3985/T

A Sunderland
on the
Mountbatten
slipway

aircraft and after finding the port propellor and reduction gear, decided to raise these along with some other artefacts and offer them to the Australian Airforce Museum. Unfortunately Neil's position finding was not as accurate as he thought it was, and it took him some time to relocate the sunken Sunderland. By this time the weather had deteriorated and silt had moved over various parts of the wreckage making orientation underwater somewhat difficult. After a lot of false starts Neil finally relocated the Sunderland's propellor and the reduction gear, and in a blaze of organization raised the lot and carted it off to R.A.F. Mountbatten for safe keeping.

Now if you or I had done this a local museum would probably have told us to go away and take our rubbish with us, but not the Australians. They were very keen to have the propellor and reduction gear for display at the R.A.A.F.'s Association's Museum at Bull Creek near Perth. After the ground engineers at Mountbatten had

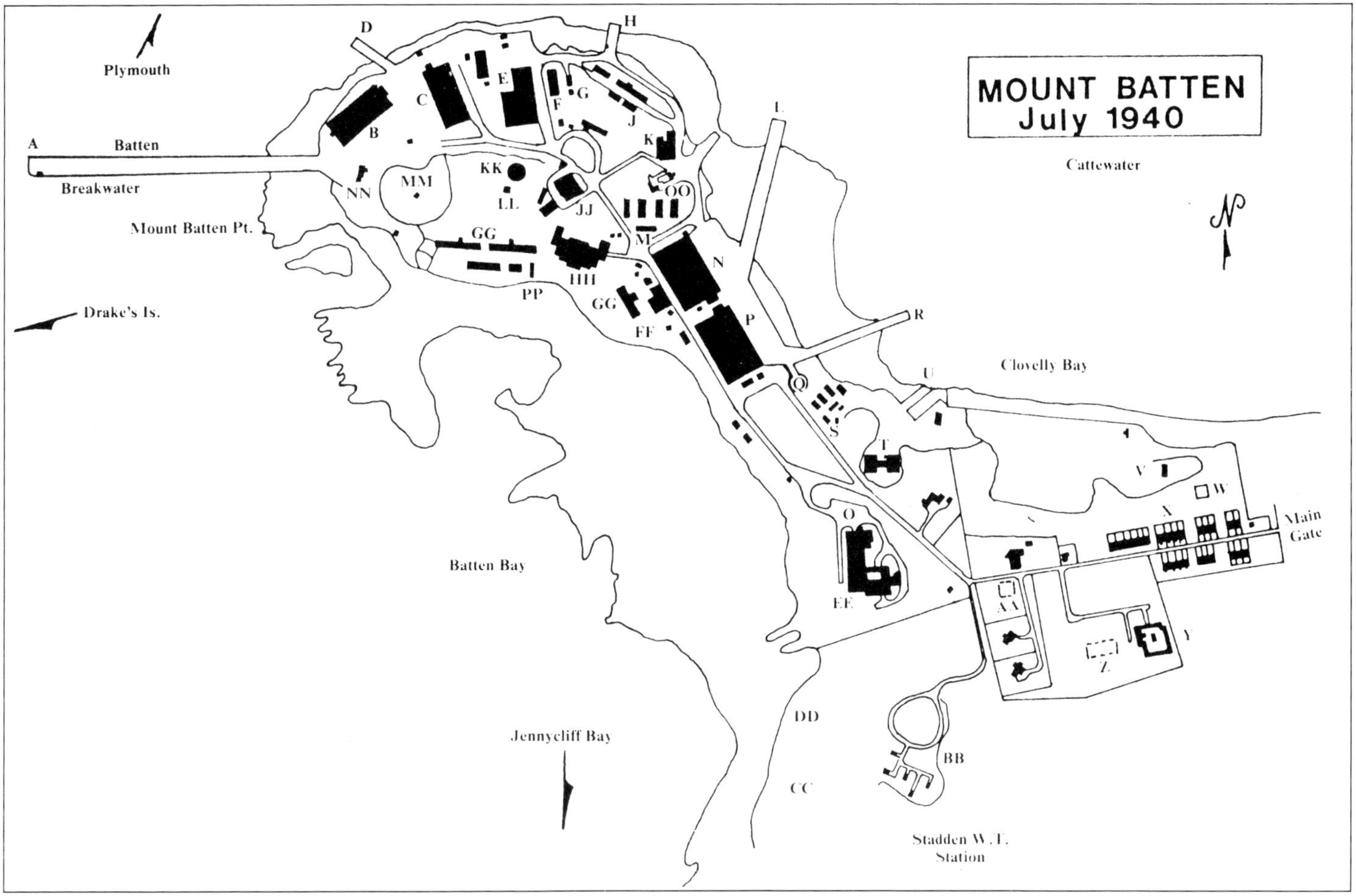

Plymouth

D H

MOUNT BATTEN
July 1940

C E G

F G J

B K

A   Batten

Cattewater

Breakwater

NN MM KK OO

LL

Mount Batten Pt. JJ M

I

GG

HH N

Drake's Is. PP GG P R

FF

Q U

Clovelly Bay

S

T

V

O W

EE AA

Batten Bay Main Gate

X

Y Z

BB

Jennycliff Bay DD

CC

Stadden W.T.
Station

N

tidied up the prop and crated it up, off it was shipped to Australia, and that is where the best bit of this story comes in. Still living in Australia were Wynton Thorpe and his flight engineer on that fateful day Jack Horgan. When the R.A.A.F. Association told them of Neil's find they were dumfounded. They had not seen each other for over forty years and so the Association invited them down to Perth to be reunited with each other, and the remains of their once proud Sunderland flying boat. You can imagine their emotion and their vivid memories of that dreadful day, and of all their lost comrades in

Plan of Mountbatten
Seaplane Station

Filters from the
recovered engine

No. 10 Squadron hangar at Mountbatten on the morning of November 28 1940

The empennage of Sunderland N9048/A was all that remained of the squadron's first Sunderland

32

10 Squadron. On May 31 1987 they stood alongside the Australian Minister for Defence and unveiled a memorial plaque at the Bull Creek Museum alongside the relics of their old Sunderland. For the two veteran survivors it was a vindication of their's and their comrades committment and sacrifice all those years ago. For Neil, unfortunately only in there spirit, it was a wonderful moment. All the effort he had put in was amply rewarded by the gratitude of the old flyers and the Royal Australian Airforce. He had discovered the wreck and returned it back to its rightful owners. Not many of us will ever get a chance to do that, especially with something that has already passed into the history books.

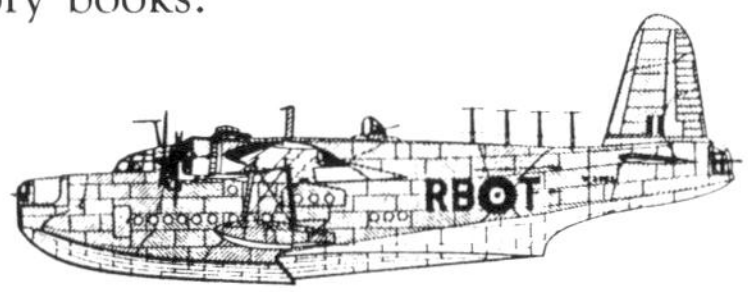

The first pieces that Neil found

Neil Griffin with the propellor he salvaged

CHAPTER 4

INTO MINES
AND ECHO SOUNDERS

The great thing about wreck diving is that however much you think you know, you can always learn more. Since I wrote Volume 1 of the Wreckers Guide I have kept diving on most of the sites and in the process have learned quite a lot more about some of them. In the case of the *Poulmic*, a completely new wreck has been discovered nearby, and interesting photographs of the crew of the *Elk* have come to light giving a unique glimpse of what their lives must have been like. At the time all of my diving partners seemed to be very interested in these developments so I thought it would be a good idea to pass these stories on. Whilst they are meant to inform and hopefully entertain, I also hope that they might encourage you to look at old wreck sites with new eyes.

The outer casing of
a mine

Lord Kelvin's Sounding Machine

Ever thought of what you would do if you did not have your trusty echo sounder? Sure you have, that's why you have it and not a pile of muddy old rope with a weight on the end. How much simpler it all is nowadays with our little electronic bunch of tricks, all we have to do is flick a switch. Not all that long ago it was all down to a leadsman stuck up in the 'chains' of a ship, calling out the marks as he labouriously threw the leaded line in front of the ship and then recovered it. Somewhere in between those two extremes were rather less well-known methods for recording depth, and one such depth machine, manufactured incidentally by Kelvin, Bottomly and Baird, who now are known as Kelvin Huges, and still make depth sounders, came to light recently on the wreck of the *Elk*.

The *Elk* was a trawlwer of some 181 tonnes built by Cook, Welton and Gommel of Hull in 1902. Requisitioned by the Navy during both World Wars, she had a checkered career and was finally sunk by a mine off Penlee Point in November 1940. When we first dived on the *Elk* she was completely intact, but over the last couple of yeas she has suffered a lot of storm damage and is starting to break up. So quite often for an evening's dive we hook into the wreck and then swim out on lines so that we have a look at the seabed all around it. In the past this has given us some nice souvenirs, mostly bottles, inkpots, door handles, and more recently a complete clay pipe. The whole area is littered with bombs and large shells, and sometimes empty brass shellcases can be found. These by the way are not from the *Elk* but from later dumping (the date is normally stamped on the bottom of the case). On one dive my partner brought up what he thought was an empty brass shellcase, but when it was cleaned up it turned out to be the business end of a small core

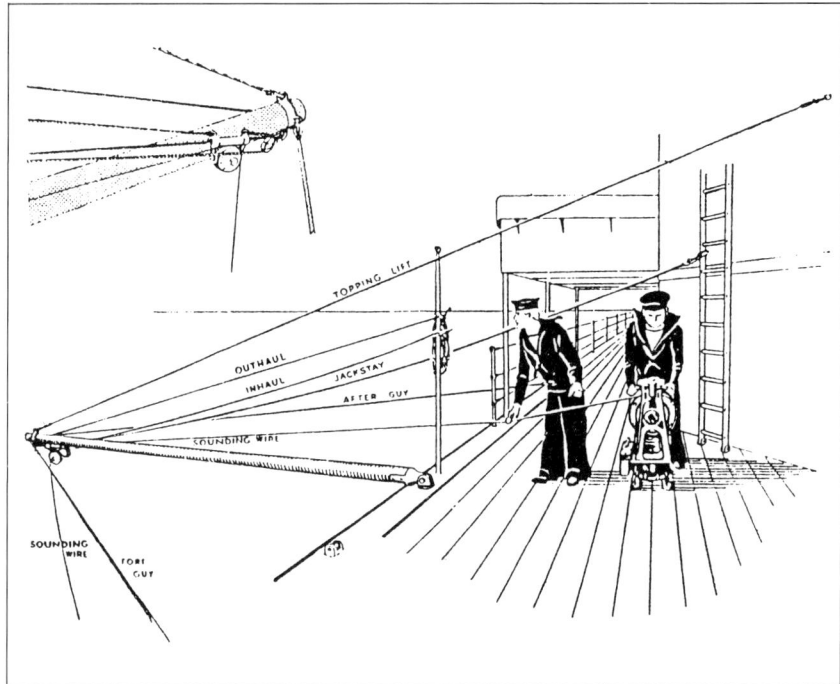

sampler. This rather mystified me until I remembered that on one dive we had come across a steel podium about three feet long, lying on its side in the sand. Could this be the winding gear? I was not convinced, or I must say very interested until Steve Carpenter, of Sound Diving at Queen Annes Battery, showed me some drawings and istructions of how to operate a Kelvin Sounding Machine that he had found in an old Admiralty seamanship manual. The whole thing looked incredible complicated with lots of wires and pulleys, and seem to need at least three men to operate it. But the machines stand was exactly like the iron one that I had seen near the *Elk*.

Now Steve is very interested in old bits of diving gear and associated machinery, so he provided the lifting bags and the boat, and we all went off on his regular evening 'swanee' dive to locate the Iron Podium. As luck would have it I managed to locate the podium on the first

Diagram showing how to use the sounding machine

sweep and very quickly my partner tied on our two lifting bags, whist I whacked in the air. As the lifting bags inflated, the podium stood up in the sand and lifted off to a height of about five feet and there it stuck. No matter how much more air we put into the bags, the wretched podium just hung there gently bobbing just above the bottom. Worse still a slight current had caught the bags and the whole contraption was slowly drifting away out of reach of our distance lines. With our time and air running low we decided to surface and get somebody else down to finish off the job. After all the podium could not get far, especially if we tied a line to it.

Having been in the services I am something of an expert at tying knots and I still maintain that my 'stokers dobyhitch' could not, under any circumstances, have come undone. Suffice it to say however, that when the next team went down, the knot had mysteriously worked loose, and the podium, complete with lifting bags had disappeared. Just as I could not believe that my knot would come undone, you dear reader, may

Far left: The crew and their children on a day out on the *Elk*

Left: Attaching a lifting bag to the 'Kelvite'

Above: Owners and crew of the *Elk*

well find the next part of this story a trifle unvelievable as well.

Six weeks later on another of Steve's Monday dives, he decided to try on the reef near the *Elk* in the hope of finding some bottles. Since there were warships exercising nearby he decided against drifting and anchored into the reef instead. As the first diver down I checked the anchor, made sure my distance line was securely fixed, and swam off. Twenty feet later I came to an abrupt halt, because there in front of me, bumbling along the reef was the missing podium still with its lifting bags attached and inflated. Wasting no time my partner elbowed me out of the way, and this time he firmly tied on the line. We surfaced, as they say in the theatre, to thunderous applause.

The rest was a bit of an anti-climax really. We got the podium into the boat and Stever carted it off to get it cleaned up. Unfortunately all the winding gear had become damaged and the podium itself was badly cracked. In the end the only useful bit was the counter on the top, which had all the measurements and its name, The KELVITE Mk IV hand sounding machine. Still with what we had, we could work out some methods of using it, and soon became glad that we never had to operate it for real. I am not a great believer in electronic bits and pieces on small boats, but after seeing the KELVITE I look at my simple Seafarer in a new light, and am glad I have it, and not the other.

The dial from the Kelvite Mk IV

The was the sounder still bumping along the bottom

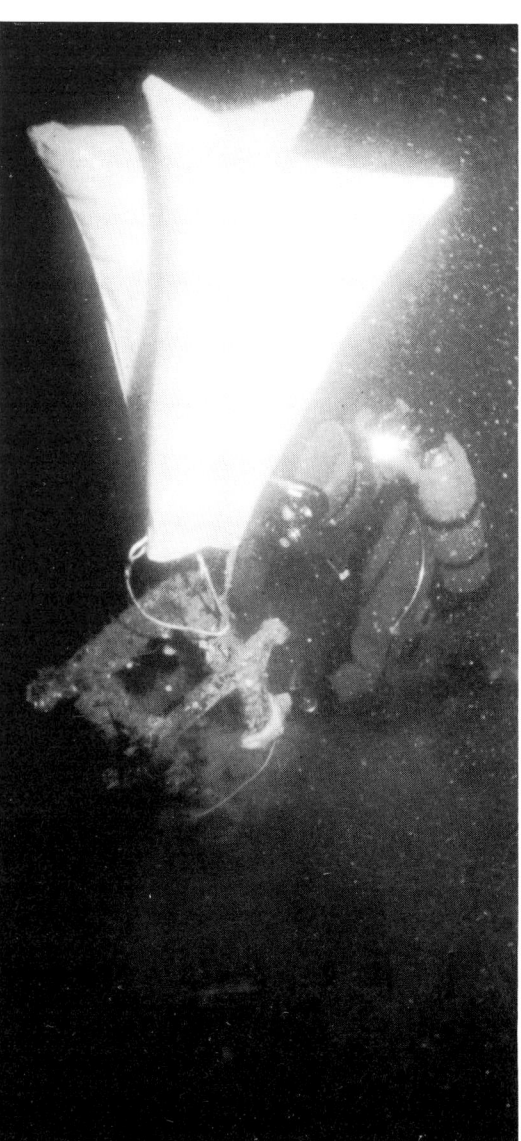

38

The *Poulmic*

MINES ON THE *POULMIC*

It always amazes me how many people seem to dive with their eyes closed. Well I do not mean acutally tight shut, just the fact that they do not see what is often right in front of them. The oft repeated cry, 'there's nothing down there' can be heard echoing all over Plymouth's wreck infested waters in the middle of the summer, and since the divers in question have usually been diving on a wreck, I sometimes wonder what they expect to find. On a wreck like the *Poulmic* for instance, a porthole or two have been found in the past, but with roughly five hundred divers a year diving on this wreck it is unrealistic to expect to find very much in the way of souvenirs.

Of course to the more committed wreck diver, every wreck is really a jigsaw puzzle waiting to be solved, and any brass, whilst always welcome, is usually considered an undeserved bonus. Most of the wrecks around Plymouth are quite straight forward. The *J. E. Layne* and the *Glen Strath Allen* for instance, are extremely well documented, but the *Penlee Cannon Site* and the *Coronation* still exert a fascination for the wreck detectives years after they have been discovered. Most people think that shipwrecks just break up and fade away, and to be truthful and awful lot do. But some like the *Ramillies* near Bolt Tail, are nearly three hundred years old and still they

Above: This 'lump' contained over 30 Bofors shells

Above right: The ammunition cleaned up and separated

live on in people's memories, and enough of their bones are left to intrigue the modern day wreck hunters. The fascination about wrecks is that they seem to link the past with the present, and however much you dive upon them, many are still capable of throwing up quite staggering surprises.

Going back to the *Poulmic* for example. I wonder how many people realize that the *Poulmic* site actually contains three different shipwrecks lying almost side by side. Surprised? Well I certainly was, especially as I quite regularly dive the *Poulmic* area, and only found out by a complete accident. In fact so recently did I find

out about them that I still am not entirely certain what they all are.

Still it just goes to show what is down there waiting to be discovered even if you think you have seen it all before.

The *Poulmic* lies about a mile off the Breakwater light, just outside the new degausing range. But it was about one hundred yards closer in that we discovered the object that was to lead us to the discovery of the other vessels. The object in question was a large mine, you know the type of thing that you see on sea fronts collecting money for distressed sailors. They are usually painted red and covered with great big prongs. We were drifting the boat at the time, just having a gentle scrap dive, with two of us hanging off the anchor rope when the anchor became snagged on a rock. When I swam along to free it, I saw that the anchor chain was happily banging up and down on a large round object half buried in a sandy gulley. The shape looked familiar, but it was only when I saw the prongs that I realised what it was. Well I can tell you that my heart certainly missed a beat or two, but almost at once I saw that there was a hole in the top and realized that after all, the mine had probably already gone 'bang'. After a good deal of careful examination the mine revealed itself to be the top half of the outer casing, presumably

40

blown off when the mine exploded during the war.

Using the mine as a start point we did a circular search of the immediate area and came up with some iron wreckage. Further dives revealed that there was more sparse wreckage which eventually led to the *Poulmic*. Now this was very interesting because we know that the *Poulmic* had been sunk by a mine during the Second World War. Was this the very mine that sunk the *Poulmic?* It certainly seemed a possible conclusion, but could it just be a coincidence? At first I was fairly certain that this was the mine, but later research showed that at least three other vessels had been sunk in the same general area during the Second World War, and that their sinkings had also been because of mines. I could see that we were going to get no easy answers to the puzzle, so we decided to lift the mine casing so that we could examine it in more detail. That's when the accident happened.

We had fixed a lifting bag onto the casing by passing a rope through the top hole and out through a small hole in the side. It all looked secure, and the bag was quickly filled with air. The mine rose gracefully off the bottom and started to accelerate upwards. Suddenly the top ring, which must have been rusted straight through, pulled out from the casing and shot towards the surface. The main body of the casing faltered, and then plunged gleefully back towards the sea bed. I was right underneath trying to take some photographs, and rapidly tried to swim out of the way. Unfortunately the casing seemed set on following me, and the chase only ended when the mine settled in a great cloud of sand inches from my fins. When the dust settled I saw that my partner was busy having hysterics, so I swam in a dignified manner back towards the anchor. It was then that I saw the remains of what looked like a stern section, complete with rudder off a small trawler. Further examination revealed ribs and more iron debris together with some broken pottery and old porcelain electrical fittings. Definately a wreck site, and definately not connected to the *Poulmic*.

So did the mine blow this vessel up instead of the *Poulmic*, or did it do for both? Well at the moment we just do not know. But that is the fun I suppose, the finding out. The answer is lying somewhere down there on the bottom, it is just a manner of interpreting correctly what we see, and drawing the proper conclusions. Other divers have found these wrecks before us, but they thought that it was all part of the *Poulmic*, because that is what they expected to see. I would have too, but luckily I found the mine, and that is what started me thinking. Looking is fun, but thinking about what you see, that's what provides the answers . . . eventually.

Attaching a lifting bag to the mine casing

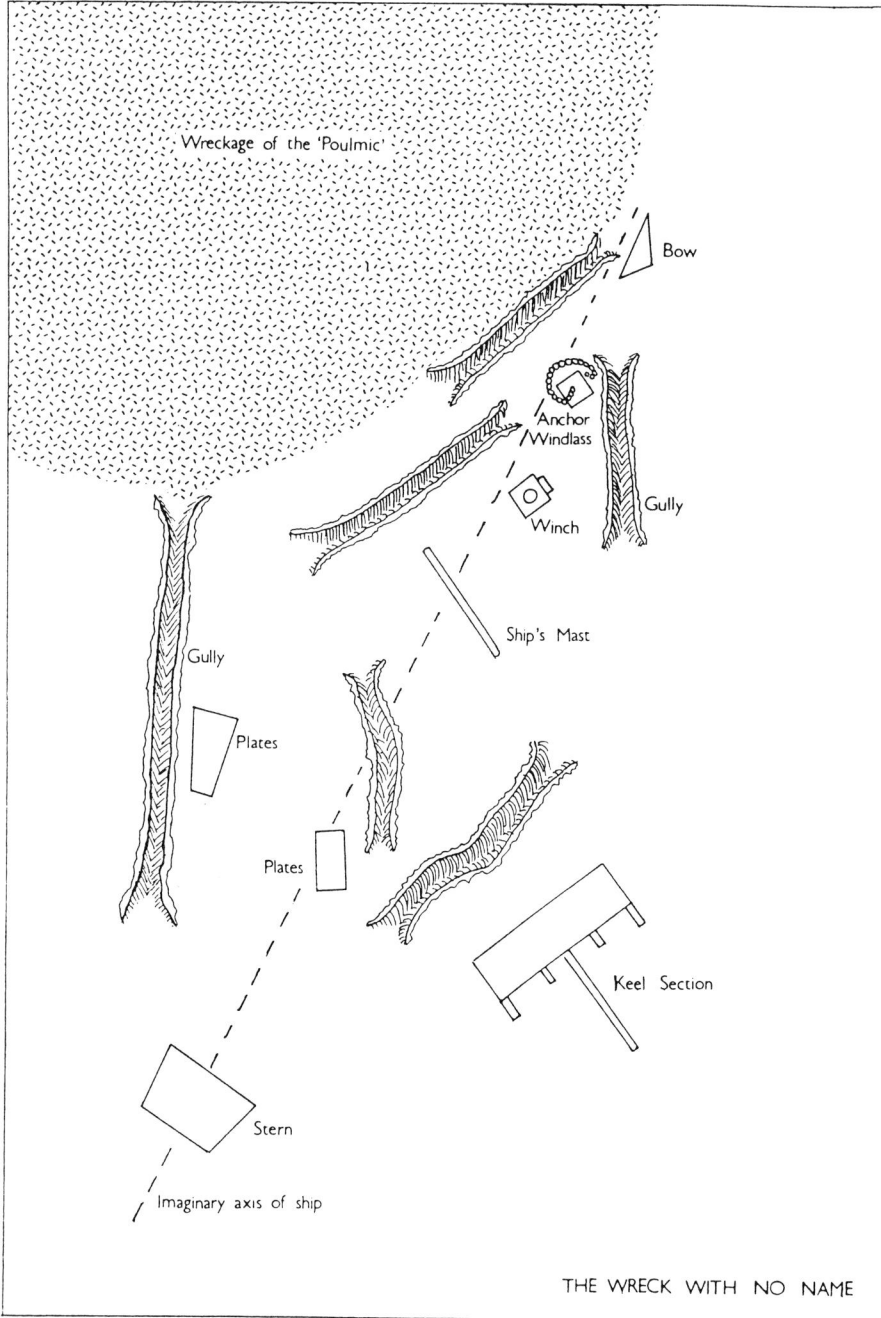

Wreckage of the 'Poulmic'

Bow

Anchor
Windlass

Gully

Winch

Ship's Mast

Gully

Plates

Plates

Keel Section

Stern

Imaginary axis of ship

THE WRECK WITH NO NAME

THE WRECK WITH NO NAME

Familarity breeds contempt. There's a cliche if ever there was one. In diving terms, maybe it's not quite so true, as familiarity often breeds confidence and competence. However in the matter of wreck diving it can also give way, after a while to a certain indifference. A good case in point is the wreck of the Poulmic, just outside the Breakwater at Plymouth. Five years ago I wrote an article on this wreck for Scene, and in the following years dived on it fairly regularly. I always enjoyed my dives, but after a while I came to think that I knew all there was to know about the wreck, and as the years rolled by I started to lose interest in it.

Because the marks for this wreck are extremely accurate, I always tend to use them religiously, and therefore always approach the wreck from the same side. Last year, quite by chance we were diving at the other end of the Poulmic wreck site when we came across the stern section of what looked like a trawler. It seemed too small to be anything to do with the Poulmic, but it could possibly be one of the many small trawlers lost in this area during the two world wars. After doing some more dives we found some ribs, lots of iron plate, and some deck fittings. I began to get 'cautiously' excited because it was becoming clear that we had found another wreck.

Now I'm quite hopeless at surveying things, it's all too long winded for me, so I enlisted the help of Roger Webber and his boat Excaliber. Roger has Decca, a magnatometer, a good ferrograph and God knows what else, and he spent a very happy day charging up and down the whole area towing his magnatometer, and chucking in marker buoys every time he got a decent reading. At the end of the day the sea was littered with marker buoys, and at last Roger turned off his magnatometer which had sounded like a demented wasp and was in danger of

driving me completely insane. When we had finished diving on all the buoys we came to the conclusion that right alongside the Poulmic lay another wreck, possibly a trawler of about 120 feet in length.

Over the next couple of weeks we dived the wreck several times but came no closer to finding out its true identity. The visibility was none too good and we kept wandering off the wrecksite onto the remains of the Poulmic. However on our next dive the weather improved immensely and we had over 50 feet visibility. As we hovered over the stern section, I suddenly saw the outline of the ship laid out before me. From ground level you would never have seen it, but from about 20 feet off the bottom it was all so obvious. Right in the middle of the wreck was a huge winch, and up front was the top end of the bows complete with anchor fairleads. Just behind the

bow was lots of anchor chain, an anchor, and scattered in the deep gullies either side were various stanchions and other deck fittings. Apart from the superstructure, here was a complete shipwreck. After diving on the Poulmic for all these years, how on earth had I never seen this wreck before? The answer, is unfortunately very simple. Because I did not know that this wreck was there, I never looked for it. I, and presumably loads of other divers kept approaching the wrecksite from the same side, and when they swam onto the new wreck they thought it was the Poulmic. Since the two wrecks almost touch at various points it would be hard to tell the difference. Anyway, why should you? It is supposed to be the Poulmic, right??

So far I have still not discovered the identity of this wreck, but my research seems to indicate that it is possibly one of two vessels sunk during

This ship is just like the *Kingston Alalite*. The *Asama* is smaller but still very similar

the Second World War. The first one is the *Kingston Alalite*. This vessel was 152 feet long with a gross tonnage of 412 tons, and hit a mine on 10 November 1940. She seems a bit larger than our wreck, but otherwise fits the bill quite well. The other vessel up for consideration, and in my view the most likely, is the Cardiff trawler *Asama*, sunk during an aircraft attack on 21 March 1941. She was 131 feet long and so is closer in size to our wreck. The trouble is that these small trawlers were sunk all over the place during the war, and usually their positions are just guestimates. The other problem is that so far nothing with any markings has been found that might give us a clue. The wreckage really only consists of the hull section, and I suspect that quite a lot of that is hidden in the sand. There is no sign of the superstructure, which is a shame because this would give us a good idea as to the builder of the vessel, and that would narrow things down quite a bit. We have now taken to drift diving off the reef that the Poulmic is on. The difference in depth is about 25 feet, and by drifting nearby, but in the direction of the Breakwater, we hope to come across some of the superstructure. If it was blown off or just came adrift, that's the way the tide and current would have taken it. So far after a whole winter's diving nothing of significance has come to light, so we are no further forward.

I said in that very first article on the Poulmic, that it was an interesting wreck. Well it certainly is that, and maybe one day I will find all the answers. One thing I certainly will not do however, and that is to become indifferent, because that seems to lead to blindness.

The bows, you can see
the anchor hawshole
quite clearly

44

The large winch in the
middle of the wreck

Mrs Pillage

THE OLD LADY AND THE BARQUENTINE

The *Yvonne*

The trouble with wreck research is that most of it is carried out in libraries, and after a while, instead of seeing the facts you just start seeing lots of dots. Much more interesting is galloping around the clifftops trying to climb down to suspected wrecksites, or gently creeping about in old churchyards, peering at grave stones in order to get an idea of all the local tragedies that have happened on the cruel sea. I much prefer being out in the open air to browsing in libraries, but you have to go where the information is, and if you are really lucky you will find a personal angle that will really make the wreck come alive. 'Eyewitness' accounts are by far the best kind of information, and if you ever see those programmes where survivors from the Titanic or some other famous wreck tell their stories, you cannot help but become interested in them and the fate of their ships. It really is compelling stuff, and I find it most surprising that many of them seem to remember events that happened seventy-odd years ago like it happened almost yesterday.

Part of my job is to help run an old people's home, and it is only fairly recently that I have realized what an untapped fund of knowledge I have right on my own doorstep. Old people, far from being disinterested spectators on life still retain for the most part an avid interest in the world that immediately surrounds them, and when they find out that you do something, that to them is downright dangerous, then their curiosity knows no bounds, especially when it comes to identifying everyday objects that have been brought up from the sea. Glass 'alley' bottles hold no mysteries for them, they are familiar objects from childhood. In one case a stone ginger beer bottle caused one old lady to shout in glee because the make 'Biscombes' was a firm that her great grandfather once owned. She was so delighted I had to give her the bottle so she could have it in her room.

Now although useful this was all pretty low-key information, until one day one of my ladies, a Mrs Pillage by name, came up to me shyly and asked if I knew anything about the wreck of a barquentine that had happened on the Plymouth Breakwater when she was a young girl. After a bit of questioning I realised that she meant the 'Yvonne' a steel barquentine of about a thousand

47

tonnes that had hit the Breakwater and sunk in August 1920. Now I did actually know this wreck and had dived on its remains quite a few times. Mrs Pillage was fascinated by this and asked me plenty of questions about how the wreck lay, and what it now looked like. She displayed such a good grasp of the situation, that puzzled she should know so much, I asked her where she had got her information from. It transpired that her grandfather had been a Harbour Pilot, and as a young girl the great love of her life had been a small sailboat. When the *Yvonne* smacked into the Breakwater she was determined to sail out there and have a look.

As she retold the story of that day her eyes sparkled with the memory, and at the end of her tale she suddenly asked me if I would like to see some photographs. There in an old envelope were three small photographs taken with an old box brownie. One showed her as a young girl in her little boat, and the other two showed the bows and stern of the *Yvonne* lying with her back broken in two on the Breakwater. You knew it was the right wreck because the little girl had taken great care to frame the stern right in the middle of the viewfinder. There in large letters was her name YVONNE.

Well I was amazed. To actually meet somebody who saw this wreck nearly seventy years ago was remarkable enough, but somebody with such clear memories certainly brought this wreck story to life in a way that the newspaper reports certainly did not. However, not content with photographs, Mrs Pillage, by now the centre of attraction, rounded off the tale of the *Yvonne* with a good old-fashioned ghost story.

It seems that the night watchmen at the wrecksite had been complaining about bloodcurling howls and the rattling of ghostly bones. Naturally enough their employers dismissed these claims as the moanings of a bunch of skyvers. However, one night things turned serious when the watchmen, although frightened out of their wits by the unearthly sounds determined to investigate. As they climed onto the wreck a steel marlin spike hurtled down from the rigging and struck quivering in the wooden deck just in front of them. Completely unnerved they fled in terror and were never seen again. Two days later Mr Turner, a sail rigger by profession, arrived at the Breakwater to collect some tools that he had recently left behind. Apparently he had been aloft to take some gear from the topmasts, and had left two marlin spikes in a bucket attached to the mast by a length of rope. As he climbed up a gust of wind blew the bucket against the rigging making a howling sound where it twanged against the ropes, whilst the marlin spike rattled from side to side in the iron bucket. Later, on his way back to Plymouth, Mr Turner was heard to complain loudly about the loss of one of his marlin spikes.

I do not know about you, but I think that's great. You just cannot get that kind of insight from files, and even if you could, it would not be the same. I have often said that wrecks are far more than just undersea scrap, they are almost living history, and it is people and their memories that provide the link that allows these wrecks to 'live' again.

Sadly Mrs Pillage died a couple of years ago, and because of her age she is probably the last person who saw the *Yvonne* lying battered and broken on the Breakwater all those years ago. But, she told me and I have told you. If you dive on this wreck you will become part of that link, and through you the *Yvonne* and her story will 'live' again. I don't know about you, but it makes me look at wrecksites just a little bit differently.

The bows of the *Yvonne*, photo taken by Mrs. Pillage in 1920

CHAPTER 5

THE WRECK OF
THE SAN PEDRO EL MAYOR

Sheltering in the shadow of Bolt Tail, the tiny village of Hope Cove is a charming reminder of what Devon must have been like at the turn of the century. During the summer hundreds of visitors swarm onto its sandy beaches and roam the rocky cliffs enjoying the almost forgotten pleasures of a truly old fashioned seaside holiday. However the person who gave Hope Cove its name did not do so idly. Over the years the Hope Cove lifeboat rescued many a poor soul from disasterous shipwrecks, and others less fortunate were often washed up more dead than alive to be fished from the sea and given shelter in some generous villagers' cottage. Over the centuries many, many ships were wrecked around Hope Cove, but only one of any note is recorded as being wrecked right inside the Cove and that was in November 1558, the year of the Spanish Armada.

The ship was the San Pedro el Mayor (St. Peter the Great) a hospital ship and part of a squadron of fourteen other large cargo hulks that came across the Channel to support and supply the galleons and fast galleys of the invading Armada. On 21 July 1558 the Spanish fleet arrived off Plymouth and the first battles took place. It soon became apparent that the smaller English ships were far more manoeuvrable than the cumbersome Spanish galleons, and this enabled them to snap at the heels of the great galleons in small, bitterly fought skirmishes which by themselves would not have beaten the Armada, but none the less caused havoc and inflicted heavy casualties amongst the Spaniards. As Drake, Hawkins and Frobrisher harried the Spanish up the Channel the San Pedro el Mayor was becoming overwhelmed with the dead and the dying. On 30 July the two fleets engaged twenty miles west of Flushing near the entrance to the river Shelt. Superior cannon fire from the British guns took a terrible toll of the Spanish vessels, but even with their disciplined broadsides the British fleet could still have been overwhelmed by the sheer might of the Spaniards' firepower. It was definitely touch and go and in the end it was not so much Drake who won, rather the English weather that made the Spanish lose. A medallion struck at the time to commemorate England's deliverance says it all. "God breathed and her enemies scattered." The gales went on for days. The British retired to more sheltered water, but for the Armada there was nowhere to go. The clumsy galleons and sluggish hulks were never much good at sailing to windward, and had to resign themselves to being blown all around the British Isles. Some sank in Scotland, some were wrecked in Ireland, and at least one, the San Pedro el Mayor, sank here on the Devon coast.

A medium sized hulk of about 550 tons, the San Pedro had a complement of about thirty sailors and one hundred soldiers, half of which were really sick berth attendants. She also carried twenty cannon, but they were more for replacements on the fighting galleons than for fighting or protecting herself. Besides general

Aerial view of Hope Cove showing 'supposed' wreck area

stores for the Armada the *San Pedro* would have carried enough medicines, food and water to make her quite self sufficient. Her general plan was to stand off from the main area of battle and have the casualties ferried out to her. Her crew would then patch them up as best they could, and later the wounded would be dropped off ashore at some friendly port. The gales and storms put paid to all that. As the *San Pedro* lurched around the British Isles food and water started to get short and water was leaking into the boat like a sieve. Conditions below must

have been indescribable. The Spaniards, unused to the freezing cold of an Orcadian winter started to die in droves and soon there were hardly enough fit people to man the vessel. As the Armada approached Ireland, the weather became even more foul, but their commanders ordered the ships not to land as the Irish had promised no quarter if any ships were wrecked on their coast. However with disease breaking out and conditions below so bad, the Captain of the *San Pedro* decided that any risk was worth taking if it meant getting out of the storms for

50

a few days, especially if he could also get some fresh water. Accompanied by the San Juan de Portugal they put into the tiny port of Vicey, hard by the anchorage of Great Blasket Island, off County Kerry. The respite was all too short. Sneaking out of Irish waters the two ships parted company. The San Juan eventually made it home to Lisbon, but the *San Pedro* would never have survived that journey. In fact by now any sort of journey was fast becoming impossible. With the gales now south westerly the *San Pedro el Mayor* once again found herself at the entrance to the English Channel. With her wounded crying out for any relief, even death, and her crew mere shambling wrecks, her Captain now knew that he had no choice but to put into port, any port, friend or enemy and then plead for help for his wounded and dying. With so few fit crew the ship was really at the mercy of the wind and tide. As she was pushed past the Scillies and up the Channel all aboard lost any hope of a safe landfall. Pounding past the Eddystone rocks in huge seas, the *San Pedro* was driven into Bigbury Bay, and at last the crew saw their only hope of salvation, Hope Cove. By now the ship was out of anyone's control. It drove straight into the Cove and smashed against a huge rock almost on the shore. (This was Shippen Rock. It supposedly got its name from this shipwreck because everyone rushed to the shore and somebody said there is a ''ship on the rock''.) The *San Pedro* still clung to life, impaled as she was on the rock. Seeing their chance forty or fifty survivors managed to escape before the ship, pounded by huge waves broke up and sank.

Four hundred years on the only reminders of these desperate events are a beam in the Village Inn at Thurlestone which they swear came from the *San Pedro*, and some gold coins found over by the old lifeboat slip. The coins check out as being the right type and period, and extensive Spanish State Papers detail in minute detail the loss of the *San Pedro el Mayor*. So where is she?

In 1960 a character by the name of George Tessyman was out spearfishing with a friend about seventy five yards from the Shippen Rock when he saw some pieces of timber sticking up through the sand. At the time he did not think much of it, but on reflection wondered if it could be part of the ''Spanish Wreck'' that was

supposed to be here abouts. Due to adverse weather conditions Tessyman did not get back to have another look for about a month, and then he looked in vain. Whatever he had seen on that spearfishing trip had now vanished beneath the sand.

To my knowledge no one else has ever claimed to have found any other wreckage, but if ever a wreck was waiting to be discovered this must surely be it. There is no doubt that the *San Pedro* ended up on the Shippen Rock, and that it was broken up by the waves. The man in charge at the time, a certain George Cary stated that ''the ship is not to be recovered, she lieth on a rock and full of water to her upper decks.'' He went on to say ''the ship I think will prove of no great

Both sides of a gold coin found near Hope Cove

51

value, the ordenance is all Iron, and no brass, their ground tackle all spent save only one new cable.'' (Calender of State Papers, Domestic, 1588.) The twenty cannon were probably all recovered, but some might still be there, the nearby Ramillies site still contains some. Also some of the crews' possessions and weapons could still be lying somewhere underneath the sand together with broken pottery from the jars that contained medicines and other supplies. There is little doubt that most of this was looted, but bits and pieces like the coins should in the end wash up somewhere on the beach. As to the wooded wreckage, well parts of the Ramillies wooden hull still survive, and that's on an exposed rocky site. In Hope Cove the sand is deep and moves all the time. Since it is almost certain that the wreck is there, it is also a fair bet that whatever is left will be quite well preserved.

Diving around the Shippen on a calm day gives you a sense of hope. The rocky bottom is crisscrossed with small crevises, just right for a coin or button to lodge in. The shoals of small fish are happy to help you poke into small clumps of brackeny weed looking for a belt or shoe buckle, and as you swim onto the sand who knows what you might find. There is little doubt in my mind that parts of the *San Pedro el Mayor* are buried under the sand. The only problem is where, and how deep. Short of vacuuming the whole sea bed around the Shippen the only answer is to wait for the storms. They released the Halloween, maybe one day they will show us the *San Pedro*, and then George Tessyman, wherever he is can say with some satisfaction, I told you so.

A Spaniards helmet

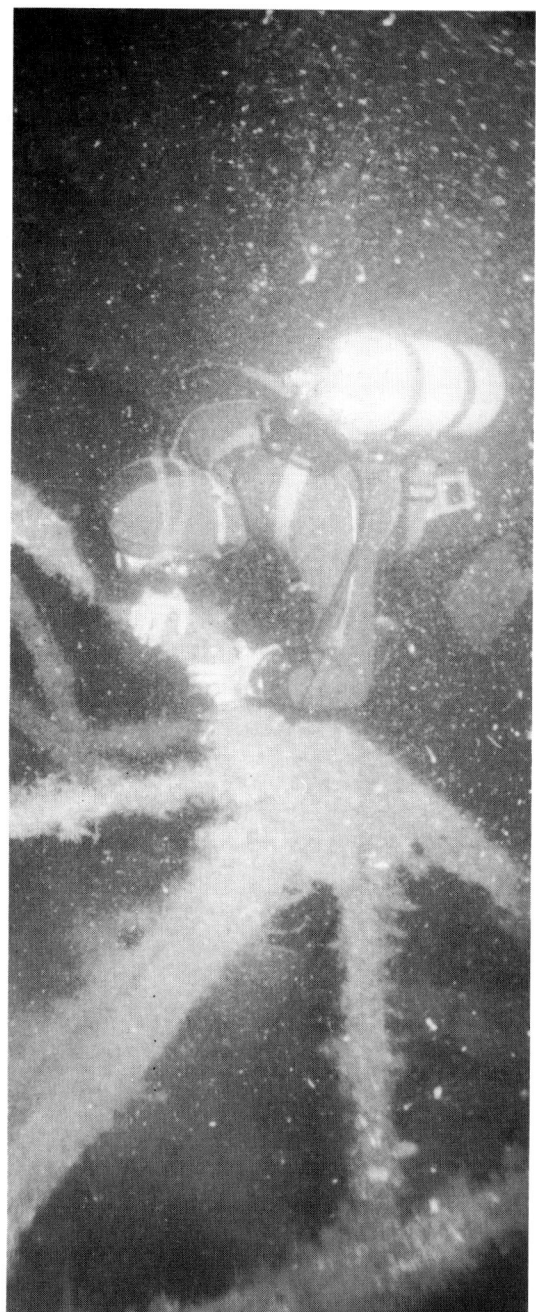

The *Maine* formerly
named the *Sierra Blanca*

CHAPTER 6

THE WRECK OF THE STEAMSHIP MAINE

I suppose all of us go through phases with our favourite divesites, and at the moment one of my favourite dives is the Maine, wrecked just outside Salcombe. I first read about this wreck way back in the 1960's when it was first discovered by the Torquay branch of the B.S.A.C. who later went on to recover its magnificent bronze prop. This was a tremendous achievement back in those days, and even now there are not many clubs that can match it. The *Maine* (she actually started life as the *Sierra Blanca*) came to a sticky end on a misty day in March 1917, when a torpedo from a lurking U boat hit her in the port side, round about her number two hold when she was about ten miles off Bolt Head. The *Maine*, a 3600 ton cargo ship,

was loaded with horse hair, goatskins, and five hundred tons of chalk, outward bound from London to Philadelphia. Very soon the holds started to fill up and Captain Johnson, after sending off distress signals, set course for the nearest land in a vain attempt to beach her. The crew of forty three must have been terrified that the U boat would finish them off, but for some reason the U boat never pressed home his attack. He was either very confident or just lost the *Maine* in the mist. In any event it did not really matter because that one torpedo was going to be enough to sink the *Maine*. As the miles drifted slowly by the *Maine* became more and more sluggish until the water level rose high enough to drown out to the engines. As the Captain

Going inside the *Maine*

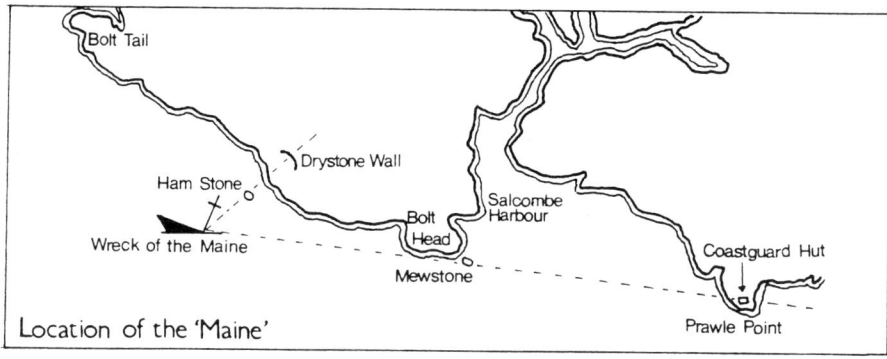

Location of the 'Maine'

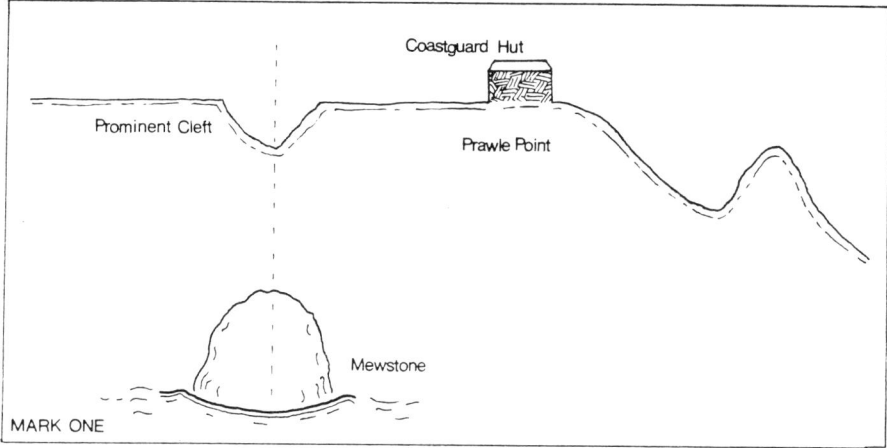

MARK ONE

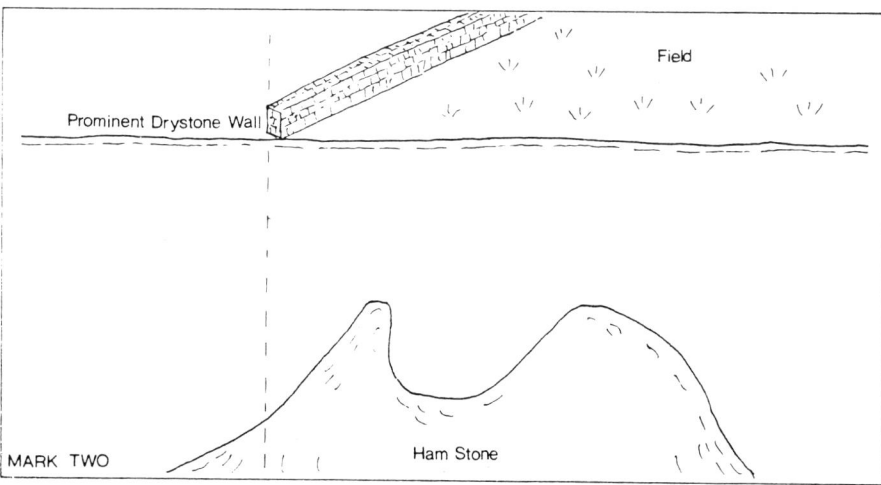

MARK TWO

ordered the lifeboats swung down and prepared to abandon ship, a Royal Navy torpedo boat appeared out of the mist and soon took off most of the crew. Because Hope Cove was by now so close, the Captain of the torpedo boat offered to try and tow the stricken steamer to safety. However by now the *Maine* was almost half full of water and the tow ropes kept parting under the terrible strain. After a while the main bulkheads collapsed, and the *Maine* sank slowly and gracefully to the bottom about two miles off Bolt Head.

Nowadays the wreck lies upright on a bed of fine shale and sand in approximately 110 feet of water, and is not as well dived as she might be. This is largely due to the fierce tidal streams that run in this area, making it impossible to dive on the *Maine* except two hours after, or two hours before high water. Even then you only have about forty minutes before the tide starts turning so you have to get it right. The marks for the wreck are very good except for the fact that the Hamstone blends in very easily with the mainland in the background. Once you pick up the marks however you just cannot miss it. A lot of people think that they have however, because they forget that the tide is now completely slack and so they sometimes have difficulty in 'hooking' the wreck in a small boat because the anchor tends to just go straight up and down. Still if you trust the marks you will be right in the middle.

Underwater the *Maine* is a fantastic sight. Because of the sandy bottom and slack water, visibility is often thirty feet or more, and the sunlight bounces up from the sea bed illuminating all the dark holes deep inside the wreck. You can swim down inside the holds and gently push your way through the shoals of pouting and pollack, then glance over the side of the hull through a myriad of fish to the sea bed below. The boilers are massive, and on top of them are large round brass valves gleaming duly in the sunlight. Down by the side of the boilers is a jumble of metal that once was the engine room. You realize this when you look through some of the gaps and see large con rods with big brass bearings on them. As you make your way towards the bows, there are other

smashed in holds to swim down into littered with scrap iron and broken railings. Small brass and copper fittings are to be found here as well, but they are all well fastened, and to be honest as soon as you see one your buddy usually distracts you by wildly waving in the direction of a better one, so it is often a case of coming up empty handed because you cannot make a decision about which bit to take off.

Mind you, in a way that is all to the good. The Maine has probably survived in such good condition because of the simple fact that it is an awkward wreck to dive on because of the tides. Often, on a smashing summers day we have been the only boat on her. Still the Maine is one of the West Country's 'classic' wrecks, and if you get an opportunity to dive on her take it, because her unspoilt condition cannot last forever.

The Barbastel winches up the Maine's bronze propellor, salvaged by the Torbay B.S.A.C.

The *Cantabria* sinking off Steeple Cove

Far right: Unfortunately this bit of wreckage was just iron

THE WRECKING OF THE
STEAMER CANTABRIA

Midway between Bolt Tail and Bolt Head lies the Hamstone, and just a few hundred yards to the east lie the towering cliffs which surround Steeple Cove. On a summers day Steeple Cove is a delightful place. The gulls and commorants glide effortlessly amid the cliff tops, and occasionally, high in the sky, a hawk can be seen hanging motionless before swooping onto its unsuspecting prey. But in the early hours of 13

December 1932, Steeple Cove was far from being a pleasant place. For surrounded in fog as it was, it nearly became the graveyard of twenty four seamen who had just been wrecked on the Spanish freighter *Cantabria*.

Heavily loaded with iron ore, the *Cantabria* was outward bound from Bilbao to Newcastle when she encountered very dense fog off the Devon coast. By early morning the Captain did not have a clue as to his exact position, and soon, almost without any warning at all the *Cantabria* ran aground on the rocks at the bottom of Steeple Cove. The crew did not have much difficulty launching their boats, and soon they had abandoned the *Cantabria* and were all heading for the shore. Unfortunately the men had not realized how steep the cliffs were, and having let go of their boats when they jumped for the rocks, they found themselves unable to climb up the cliffs or get back into the lifeboats.

It was into this potentially disasterous situation that the Salcombe lifeboat came after painfully groping her way along the coast in thick fog. By now a heavy ground swell had started up and it had become far too dangerous for the lifeboat to approach the rocks upon which the *Cantabria's* crew were trapped. The coxswain of the lifeboat however was not short on initiative, and after making the lifeboat fast to the wrecked steamer, he went on board and found a small boat which had been left behind. Using this boat the lifeboat's crew, after making over a dozen journeys, managed to get all twenty four people off the rocks and safely into the lifeboat.

By now it was obvious that the combination of a very heavy cargo and a severe ground swell spelt the end for the *Cantabria*. With the continual pounding she eventually went to pieces and soon disappeared beneath the waters, leaving the Cove once more occupied by only the seabirds and the hawks.

Over the years Steeple Cove has not changed very much and the wreckage of the *Cantabria* lies almost exactly where she originally ran aground. The photograph shows her position very clearly, and right at the foot of these rocks is where most of the wreckage lies. For a wreck in only thirty five feet of water the *Cantabria* is really impressive, and can rival many wrecks in deeper water. Unfortunately the *Cantabria* was a cheaply built ship and so there is not much in the way of brass or copper. Her propellor for instance, is still there lying on the rocks, but before you all get too excited let me tell you that it is just a common old iron one. Even so this sort of find certainly sets the scene for this wreck. The great majority of the wreck is to be found at the foot of the pinnacle rocks shown in the photograph.

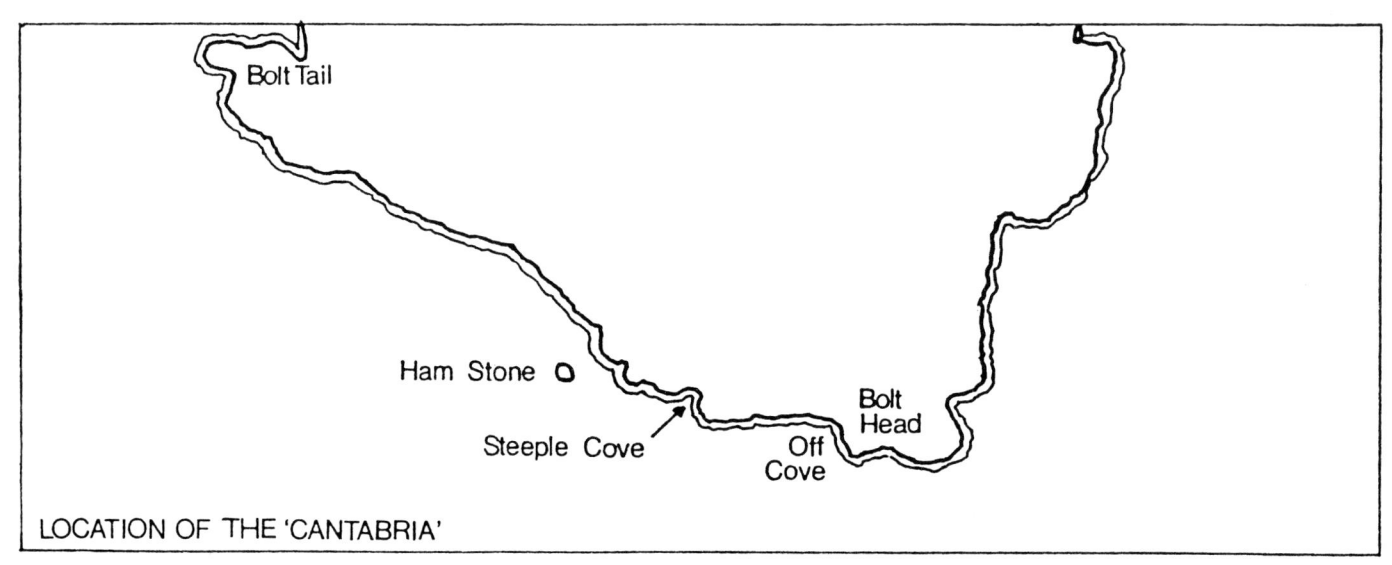

LOCATION OF THE 'CANTABRIA'

Underwater these rocks have fairly broad flat bases which gently fall onto the sand. The boilers, still reasonably intact, lie here surrounded by rusty iron plates and sections of broken guardrail. Up on a rocky plateau lies the iron propellor, with a large section of decking stretching out across the rocks. Underneath this is a large amount of debris which is well worth poking about in, as sometimes a small brass fitment such as a porthole fastener can be found. Lying across the decking and supported by another rock are the remains of the propellor shaft. This is in quite good condition and will lead you over the other side of the rocks where some more, smaller amounts of wreckage lie scattered. Going back to the main parts of the wreck, further inspection will reveal that large amounts of the decking are most probably the main deck and the one below compressed together, and in some places holes reveal an interior which goes down some four or five feet. A few yards away from the boilers lie one of the Cantabria's anchors with some chain attached. As you swim away from this towards the other end of Steeple Cove, more small pieces of wreckage can be seen and in the jumble of rocks at the base of the cliffs more anchor chain is to be found, as well as other pieces of iron plating crudded into the rock. You can spend a great deal of time looking around these rocks, because you get the feeling that just behind the next one something really exciting is waiting to be found.

All in all the Cantabria is a very underrated wreck site. There is certainly plenty to see, and the underwater scenery is far from boring. With its shallow depth there is no need to whip around it, and the inquisitive diver can indulge himself by taking plenty of time and really enjoy himself.

I suspect that if this wreck was located in deeper water many more divers would flock to it. Still a wreck is a wreck whatever depth of water it lies in. So next time you are in this area make time to give this one a dive. You will not be disappointed.

Far left: The weed encrusted boilers of the Cantabria

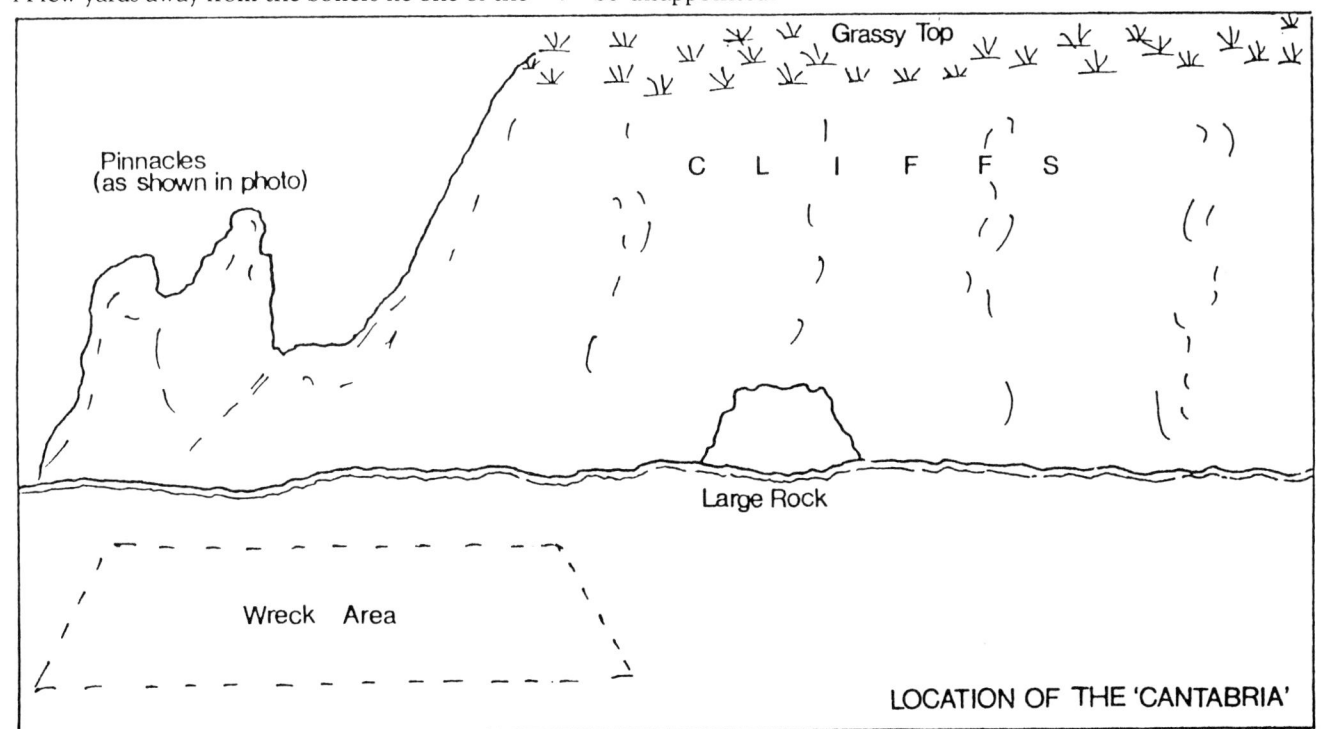

Pinnacles (as shown in photo)

Grassy Top

C L I F F S

Large Rock

Wreck Area

LOCATION OF THE 'CANTABRIA'

The steam drifter *Charter*

The steamer *Jane Rowe*

THE WRECKING OF THE CHARTER
AND THE JANE ROWE

Between Bolt Tail and Bolt Head lie five miles of the most trecherous coastline anywhere on the South Devon coast. Over the years shipwrecks have carpeted this part of the coastline almost end to end, and some have become so jumbled together that it is hard to tell where one starts and the other ends. The area underneath Bolberry down, near Catehole cliff is a good example of this chaos, because at the bottom of the steep cliffs lie the remains of two ships, separated in their wrecking by nearly twenty years, but now lying almost inextricably entwined together in the shallow seas.

The first vessel to be wrecked here was the *Jane Rowe*, a former Cardiff collier now owned by a firm in Gefle, Sweden. Built by Palmers of Newcastle, she was launched in 1889 as the *Mary Thomas* but later changed her name to *Barto* when she was sold to another firm, and finally, after being sold again to the Swedish company, she was renamed the *Jane Rowe*. During February 1914 the *Jane Rowe* loaded up in Oran with three thousand tons of burnt ore bound for Rotterdam. In the early morning of the 28 February, the *Jane Rowe*, surrounded by dense fog 'somewhere off Salcombe' ran gently aground on the only sandy

61

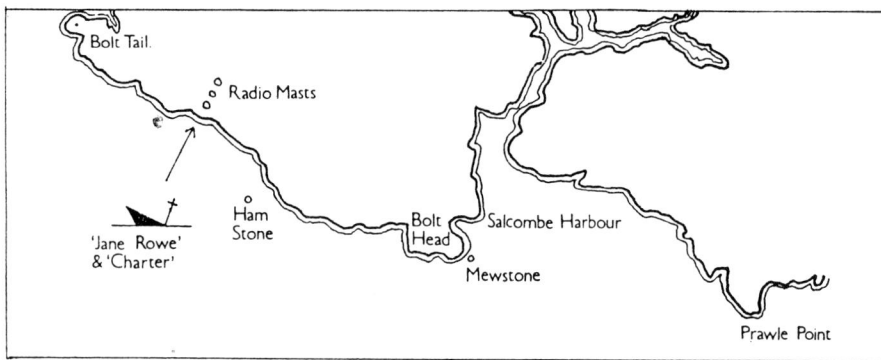

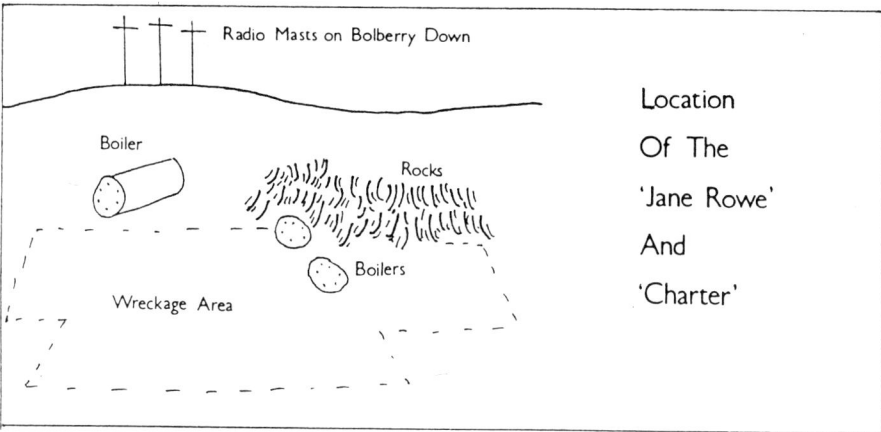

Location
Of The
'Jane Rowe'
And
'Charter'

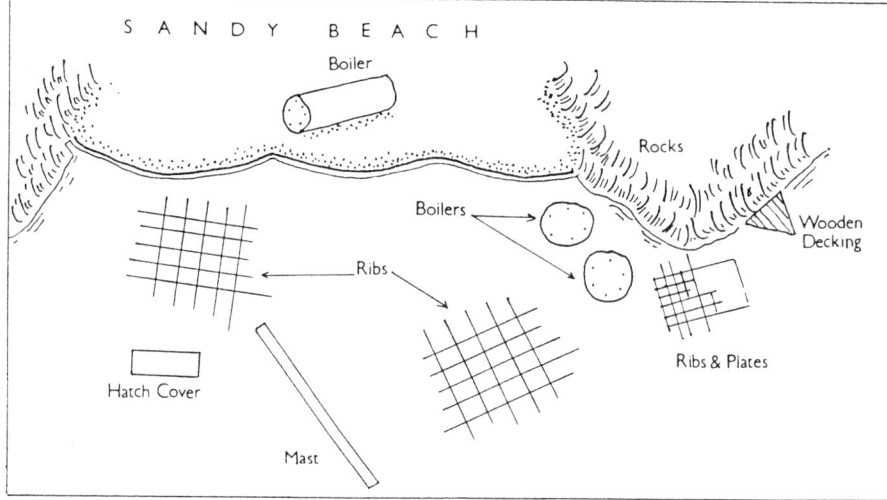

bit of beach for miles around, right under Bolberry down golf links about a mile and a half east of Bolt Tail. Shortly after dawn the wreck was sighted by the Kingsbridge Packet, a small steamer which plied between Plymouth and Salcombe. She closed the grounded steamer and passed her a tow but in the end could not budge her, and left to summon some tugs. Meanwhile a pair of early morning rabbit catchers had seen the wreck and notified the Coastguard who launched a lifeboat from Hope Cove. However when they arrived there was very little they could do except wait until the tugs arrived about three hours later. Whilst the lifeboat stood by, five tugs tried until half past nine at night to refloat the *Jane Rowe*, but to no avail. When the lifeboat and the tugs returned the next morning they found that the tide had pushed the stricken vessel further up the sandy beach, and that she was now lying broadside at the base of the cliffs. The weather had by now changed for the worse, and huge waves were breaking right over the ship, pounding the hull up and down on the beach. As the day wore on the *Jane Rowe* started to develop some serious leaks and it became clear that she was not going to survive. Since the lifeboat could not get close enough to the vessel to take the crew off, and the crew steadfastly refused to jump into the huge surf and swim to the lifeboat, the rocket brigade was sent for. A line was fired from the top of the cliffs and secured high up in the *Jane Rowe's* foremast, and a breeches buoy was swiftly rigged. Eventually all the crew were safely pulled off the wreck, including the ships kitten, a cat, and lastly a very large dog that nearly did for the crew member struggling to save him. After a while, the *Jane Rowe*, now a total loss, began to break up and by the time the year 1933 came along she had all but disappeared, with only her boilers left to mark her going. Once again the stage was set and the little piece of sandy beach was ready to receive its next victim which turned out to be the Lowestoft drifter the *Charter*, which had been fishing out of Plymouth.

Once again fog was the culprit, laced with a small amount of over confidence, which caused the *Charter* to run aground on the afternoon of 7 January on a full tide. There was an aggravating

begin to break up and her wreckage mingle with the rusting remains of the *Jane Rowe* until eventually they would be as one.

Nowadays it is very easy to sail straight past the little sandy beach as the boilers have blended very well into the background. However as the tide ebbs a small boiler is clearly visible lying in the middle of the sand, and over to the right on a rocky ridge you suddenly realise that the rocks are of too regular a shape, and you then see the two other boilers which are much bigger and therefore probably come from the *Jane Rowe*.

It is probably best to wait till near high tide to explore the rest of the wreck as it is all extremely shallow, and has an irritating ground swell at low tide. Because it is so shallow you really only need a snorkle to find the main points of the wreck and this makes it very suitable for youngsters and non diving wives. Right in front of the beached boiler are the stern ribs of the hull of the *Jane Rowe* lying across the beach. Quite often these are covered in sand and not always visible, as is a large piece of mast some fifteen feet long, and part of a deck house which is nine tenths buried in the sand a little further out. Other pieces of plate can sometimes be found, but I think it would be fair to say that most of the *Jane Rowe* is now buried somewhere down in the sand. However over to the right of the beach stand the other two boilers, one upright and the other lying on its side. As the swell hits these, water gets trapped inside the boilers and is then explosively forced out through small holes in the iron plating making a noise like a sounding whale and heaving a fine mist of spray into the air. Further around smashed into the rocks are the remains of the *Charters* bows (I think) and various other pieces of wreckage that continue along the bottom of the rocks and into the next little inlet. Everything is well smashed up but it is interesting to try and piece it all together, and also to try and separate the two wrecks. The thing about these wrecks is that you never know for certain which one you are on, so if you like crosswords or puzzles this is the place for you.

In any case it is a very beautiful area, and on a flat sunny day an extremely pleasant dive. Anything else has got to be a bonus.

A boiler hard up on the beach

ground swell and a fresh wind blowing up which drove the fog away, but the well built trawler lay comfortably on the sandy beach. Comfortably that is until the tide started to ebb and caused the trawler to fall over on her beam ends. The crew, ten in all, had by now vacated the *Charter* and were stood around unconcernedly on the beach waiting to see if they could refloat their boat on the next tide. The lifeboat, this time from Salcombe, had arrived to stand by the vessel, but soon saw that she was not going to be needed. Unfortunately when the next high tide arrived it became obvious to the crew that the *Charter* was beyond refloating, and all they could do was salvage whatever equipment they could. Once more the beach had claimed another ship, but thankfully no lives had been lost on either occasion. Soon the *Charter* would

The *Blesk*
hard aground

THE WRECK OF THE OIL TANKER BLESK

The Torrey Canyon, Amoco Cadiz, and the Exxon Valdez are all infamous for one thing, oil pollution. In the mid 1800's that phrase had no meaning at all, and if you had told people that a hundred years later oil pollution would be one of the world's worst problems, they would probably have said, so what. You cannot really blame them, afterall they had enough problems of their own. Nowadays we all complain about cars polluting the atmosphere, but imagine London in the horsedrawn 1850's. With a population of well over two and a half million, there were up to a million horses working in England's capital city depositing something like sixteen thousand tons of horse dung on the streets every day. Just imagine it. Give me good old carbon dioxide any day. Still as the internal combustion engine started to replace the horse, petrol became more and more in demand and soon ships were being specially designed to transport it. The controversial age of the oil tanker had dawned.

One of the first ships to be specially designed for oil shipments was the Russian steamer *Blesk*, and she was to have the unhappy distinction of being the very first oil tanker to be wrecked on the coast of the British Isles. 298 feet long, and loaded with 3180 tons of petro-oil, the *Blesk* was built to have all her holds at the front and her engines at the stern. Defying the convention of the times her bridge and accommodation was set well back towards the stern instead of being placed amidships. This first design was almost right first time and did not really alter until the first of the supertankers came along in the early sixties.

On November 14 1896 the *Blesk* left Odessa bound for Hamburg. On 1st December the *Blesk* was at the entrance to the English Channel and Captain Adolph Deme, confident in his navigation, cracked on at the *Blesk's* full speed which was around ten knots. It was a thick, dark day with heavy rain, and when Captain Deme saw a light blinking ahead in the murk he consulted his chart and decided that he was about to pass the Corbiere light just off Jersey. As he altered his course to come slightly more to the north it never occured to him that the light was actually coming from the Eddystone Lighthouse. By altering course Captain Deme had now aimed the *Blesk* straight at the coast of Devon. As the rain continued its downpour the afternoon drew into the darkness of night, and the visibility dropped to nil. But still Captain Deme, happily pacing his bridge had no idea of the impending disaster that was shortly to happen. At just after nine o'clock that evening the *Blesk*, still forging ahead at ten knots, ran full tilt into the Greystone rock and ran hard up onto the Greystone Ledges just to the east of Bolt Tail. Because she had hit so hard and ridden up over the Ledges, it was fairly obvious even at that early stage that the *Blesk* would never get off.

Captain Deme ordered flares and distress rockets to be launched, and opening the ships firearms locker issued hanguns to his officers and told them to fire those as well. With the seas pounding her stern, and the noise of her hull grating and banging on the rocks, it must have been a terrifying time for all the crew. However they all kept their heads and nobody tried to commit certain suicide by attempting to jump ship. At last the Hope Cove lifeboat appeared, and in the space of two trips managed to save all forty three crew and take them to the safety of Hope Cove. By the next day the *Blesk* was a total loss with her oil gushing into the sea. In those days it was a rarity to see oil floating on the water and people came from miles around to stand on the cliff tops and watch the oil stain the sea black all along this part of the coast. After a while however the novelty wore off as the fumes made people vomit, and the stench grew horrendous. Local reports at the time said that you could smell the oil in Totnes, over twenty miles away. As the oil spread it poisoned all the fish between Bigbury and Prawle Point, and soon every tide brought ashore oiled up lobster, crabs, bream and mullet, all killed by the *Blesk's* escaping cargo. It was a sad time for Hope Cove and Salcombe, and a glimpse of the ecological catastrophies yet to come.

Today if you swim around the Greystone Ledges the one thing you will not find is any wreckage belonging to the *Blesk*. However if you swim along Redrot Ledges, which are more towards Bolt Tail, you will come across plenty of boiler coke, solidified lumps of tar, and a certain amount of wreckage. It's my belief that here in about thirty five feet of water lie the remains of the *Blesk*. Thick kelp cover the area and a ground swell can build up very quickly throwing the unwary diver against the larger rocks that lie closer inshore. There is not much to see because only the bow is here and that is

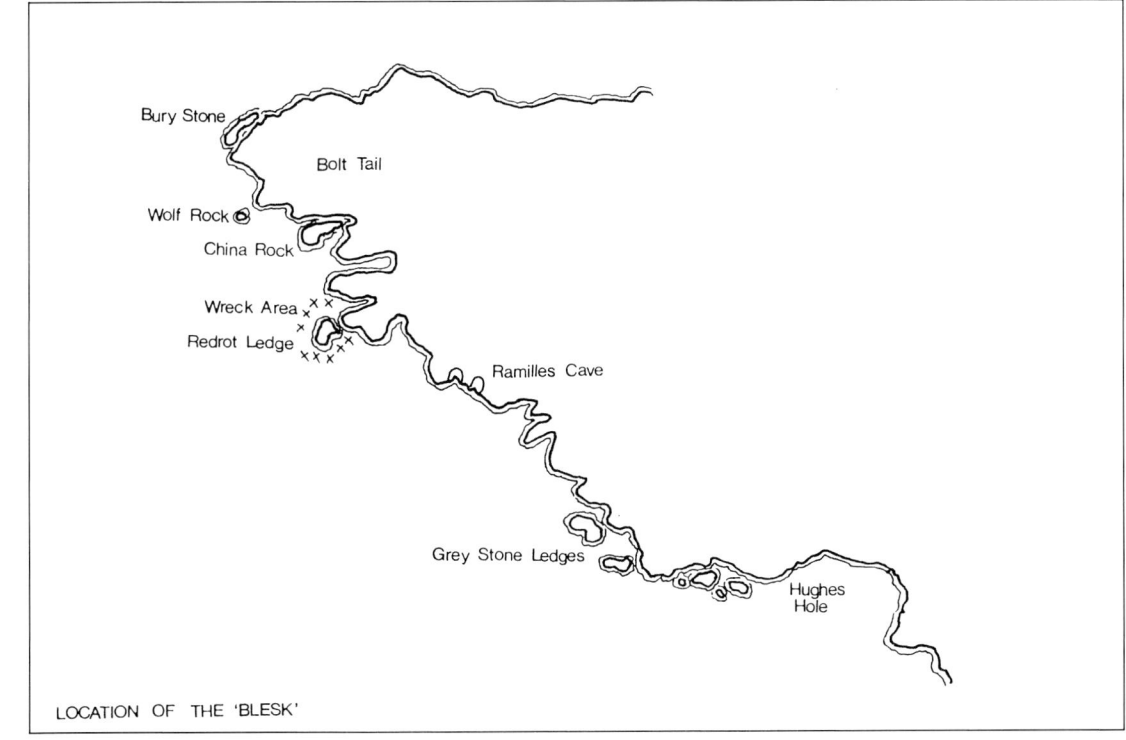

LOCATION OF THE 'BLESK'

smashed to pieces. Only bits of iron plate, part of a hatch and pieces of guardrail are to be found, along with what looks like part of the foremast's loading boom. Most of the wreckage is in the inlet towards Bolt Tail and forms a little bay just to the left of the ledges, but if you look hard you will find small bits and pieces on either side of the ledges, but closer in towards the base of the cliffs.

So why is the *Blesk* not on the Greystone Ledges? Well I am afraid that I just do not know. All the reports of her standing give the Greystone Rock or Ledges as the place that she struck, but the fact is that no trace of the *Blesk* or any other wreck can be found in the area. In desparation I had a magnatometer scan done of the whole area, from the bows of the Jebba right around to Hughes Hole, but absolutely nothing turned up. Whilst I am happy to be proved wrong I can only assume in the meantime that the reports were mistaken. The two areas are pretty close together, and in the photo of the *Blesk*, Redrot Ledge looks a better bet than the Greystone. But then it is not a high definition photograph. Still if the wreckage is the *Blesk* then where is the rest of her?

Well there are many reports of more wreckage about two hundred yards west of Bolt Tail, but I have never had any confirmation. I have had a look myself but with no luck, but that does not mean it is not there. Judging by the rest of the wrecks in this area the stern should be somewhere near by, probably buried in the sandy bottom. I have been hoping to run a magnatometer over where I think the missing wreckage is, and who knows maybe this will turn up some clues as to where the resting place of the *Blesk* is.

If from this account you think that the site is not worth visiting then you would be wrong. Like all of this area, the scenery is dramatic, the bird life fantastic, and the shallow water diving excellent especially on calm days when visibility can be in excess of fourty feet. You might not find much of the *Blesk*, but you can enjoy yourself trying.

THE WRECK OF THE LIBERTA

All along South Devon, the coast is dotted with various outcrops of rock called 'Mewstones', and because they invariably stand at the entrance to busy ports or harbours, each one seems to have its own crop of shipwrecks. The pair of Mewstones standing guard outside the entrance to Salcombe Harbour are no exception, and since they lie in the middle of a particularly notorious stretch of coastline, (Bolt Tail to Prawle Point) it is remarkable that many more ships have not been smashed to pieces on their uncompromising rocks.

In 1926 however, on a foggy February Sunday evening, the Mewstone was about to claim its first victim for some years, the Italian steamer *Liberta*. The *Liberta*, a 375 foot steamer of some 4073 tons had been built by Barclay Curle of Glasgow in 1900 as the *Vermont*, and was on her way from Spezia to Rotterdam in ballast. The intention of her master, Capt. Achille Moscatillii was to pick up a cargo of coal and return to Italy. Unfortunately for him he ran foul of the English Channel's weather, and ended up blundering along the coast of Devon completely lost. On Sunday, February 14, Capt. Moscatilii not only had fog to contend with, but a south westerly gale that blew his ship unearingly towards the rocky coast near Salcombe. In an effort to fix his position in the dense fog the crew took frequent soundings, and since these showed a consistent depth of over twenty fathoms, they assumed that all was well and they they were well south of where they actually were. Whilst they were all no doubt congratulating themselves on their good fortune the *Liberta* quietly ran aground, passing inside the Little Mewstone and the shore, ending up stuck between both Mewstones. There was very little panic as the gounding had been quite gentle, however the problem was, where on earth were they? The Capt. sent out a distress call on his radio and also sounded his siren in long mournful blasts. The crew waited paitently. Soon the wind started

to blow more fiercely, the ran lashed down in sheets, and the sea, whipped up by the now gale force winds, funnelled in through the Mewstones, the waves breaking right over the *Liberta's* deck. The Italian crew began to become increasingly uneasy.

Luckily the *Liberta's* distress call had been picked up by a 'ham' radio enthusiast at South Sands, and although he could not pinpoint the exact location, he telephoned the Coastguard at Prawle Point who decided that the wreck must be near Bolt Head. They immediately phoned the Hope Cove lifeboat which launched in truly awful conditions, and took over four hours to row the five miles to Bolt Head in the pitch dark, arriving just before dawn.

Meanwhile other radio stations had picked up the *Liberta's* signals and decided that the strickened vessel was really off Start Point, so the Torbay lifeboat was launched as well. Fortunately this one was motorised, and the coxswain, finding no wreck off the Start used his

Above: Breeches buoy on the *Liberta*

Left top: Piece of hatch stuck in the rocks

Left bottom: Redrot ledge looking towards Bolt Tail

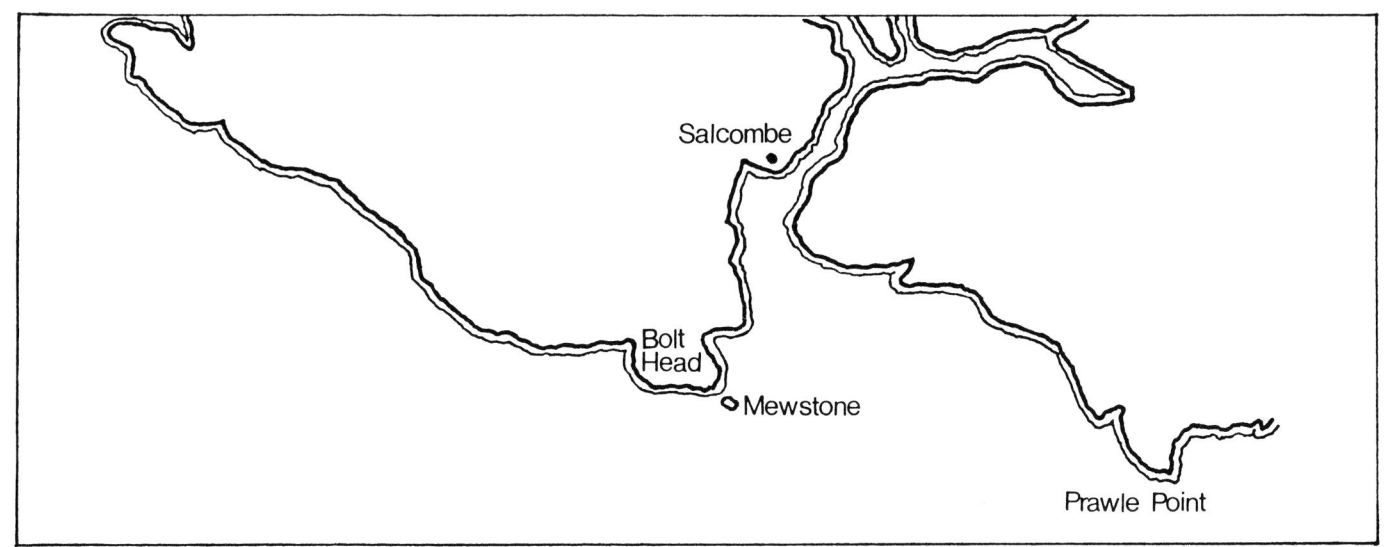

Salcombe

Bolt
Head

○ Mewstone

Prawle Point

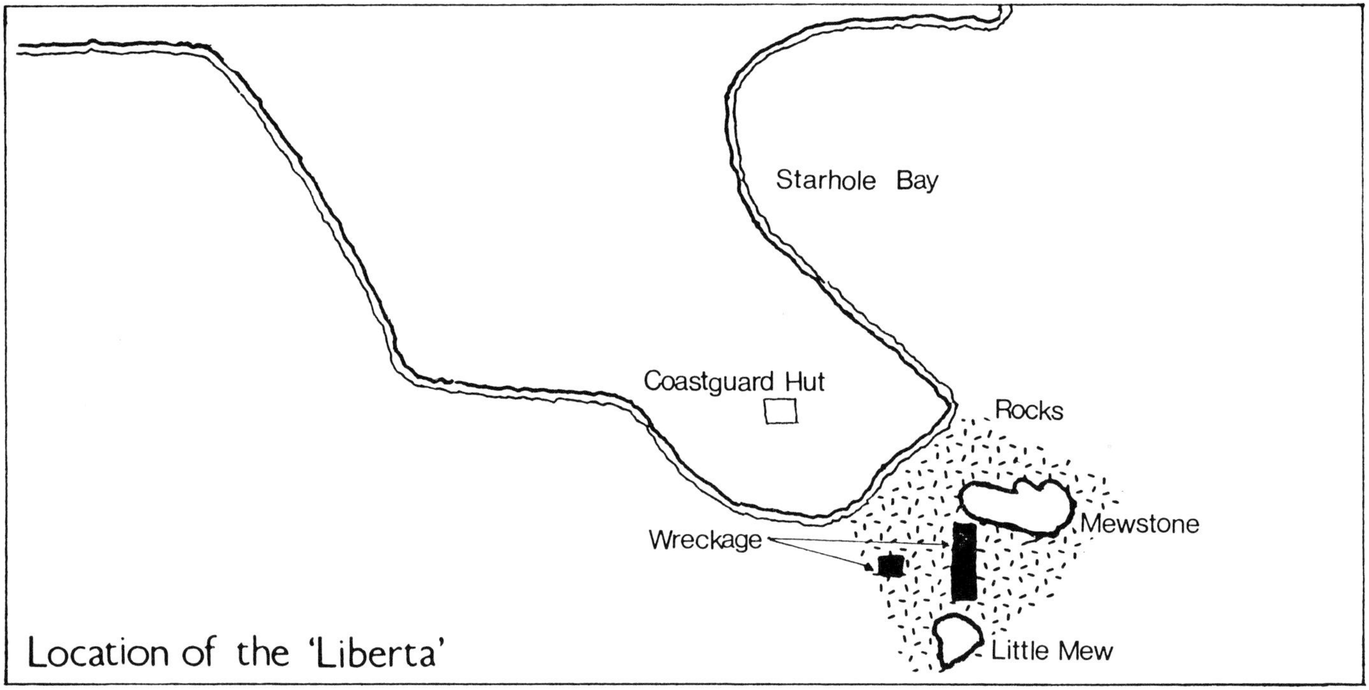

Starhole Bay

Coastguard Hut

Rocks

Wreckage

Mewstone

Little Mew

Location of the 'Liberta'

common sense and continued on past Prawle Point and on to Bolt Head. It was just as well, because by now the Hope Cove lifeboatmen were exhausted, and in the first pale light of dawn it was obvious that they had no hope of getting anywhere near the wreck as she was jammed on a large rock, and as each wave washed over her she plunged up and down like a giant see-saw. As the fog lifted the Torbay lifeboat hove into view, and the two coxswain decided to wait until the light got better so they could properly assess the situation. By now the steamers crew could just make out the two lifeboats, and feeling that they were going to be abandoned, they started to fire off distress rockets and called despairingly to the lifeboatmen for help. The Torbay boat, at some considerable risk moved in very close to the wreck and tried to reassure the crewmen. This however just made them more panicky, and in the end a buoy and line was rigged between the two vessels. With great difficulty three men were dragged off the deck of the Liberta, through the heaving sea to the comparative safety of the lifeboat. The rest of the crew, horrified at the dangers involved, thankfully turned for their salvation to the Hope Cove Rocket Apparatus Team which conveniently turned up in the nick of time and rigged a breeches buoy from the clifftop to the deck of the Liberta. Not only did they rescue all the remaining crew, they also managed to save the ship's cat and dog as well.

Four days later the Liberta broke in half, and very shortly afterwards she disappeared beneath the waves forever.

The Liberta breaks in two

69

Part of the *Liberta* bow section near the Big Mewstone

swim against, so take precautions. As you would expect the *Liberta* is well broken up, but there are still some very big bits of her left. Her boilers for instance are still quite recognisable, and lie further in towards the line of rocks that form a sort of bar at the western edge of the Mewstones. After you have swum around the wreckage for a while you start to recognise bits and pieces amid the jumble of steel plate, like the masts for the derricks, parts of the cargo hatches, and the empty sockets where once portholes were lodged.

Closer in towards the Great Mewstone, parts of the hull are perched on top of the rocks to that you can peer underneath, and in places it is possible to wriggle inside parts of the hull, but if you are a bit on the large side I would give it a miss. Although I have only seen one, other divers tell me that good sized lobsters are fairly common. Much more interesting to my mind are the pollock which hunt the sand eels. If the sun is shining you can see clouds of these little silver sand eels silhouetted against the surface, wheeling like fighter squadrons as the pollock tear into the attack. It really can be quite spectacular.

The *Liberta* is not one of the great wreck experiences, nor is it particularly scenic. But its location is very impressive and the wreckage interesting enough to keep most people happily occupied. As a second dive it is ideal, and on a sunny summers day, I for one can quite happily dive on it all day.

Today the *Liberta* lies more or less exactly where she sank all those years ago. The area between the two Mewstones and the shore is a nightmare of trecherous rocks and violent currents, but if you wait for a calm day, slack water, and preferably low tide (so that you can see all those rocks that would otherwise be hidden), you can just sail straight into the middle of all those rocks and drop anchor. You will hook immediately because you will be right in the middle of the *Liberta's* bow section.

The sea bed here is very rocky with large patches of sand, and a fair amount of weed. The depth is only about thirty feet so you have plenty of time to look around. But remember, once the tide starts turning it can become too strong to

The *Halloween* under full sail

CHAPTER 7

SOAR MILL COVE
GRAVEYARD OF THE CLIPPERS

The *Halloween*
hard aground in
Soar Mill Cove

Halfway between Bolt Head and Bolt Tail lies *Soar Mill Cove*, guarded to the south by the Hamstone which has been the cause of so many wrecks in this area. The Herzogin Cecilie struck the Hamstone as did the Soudan, and in 1881 the Volere, an Italian barque with a cargo of marble was driven into *Soar Mill Cove* and dashed to pieces almost in the same place as the Lintor Kent, also supposed to be carrying marble in 1765.

However the wreck that *Soar Mill Cove* is famous for is the *Halloween*, which ranked with the Herzogin Cecilie as one of the most beautiful and fastest clippers of her day. Whilst the Hertzogin Cecilie got away from *Soar*, and for a while looked as if she would fight another day, the *Halloween* was doomed from the very first moment she struck. Either way *Soar Mill Cove* did for both of them, and that's why I call this place the graveyard of the clippers.

The *Halloween* hard aground in Soar Mill Cove

THE WRECK OF THE HALLOWEEN

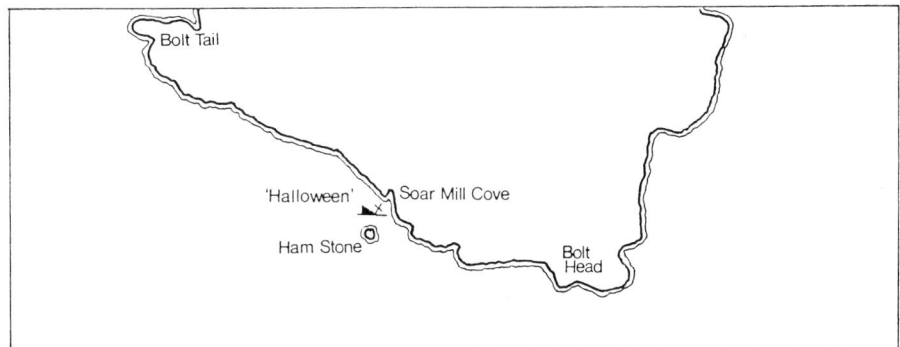

If there is one quality that a wreck diver should have in abundance it is the ability to think positive. So many times divers give up on good potential wreck sites because they become discouraged all too quickly, and then talk themselves into believing that the wreck is not there anyway. It is all too easy to do especially when under pressure from your diving buddies to get on to a 'proper' wreck and stop fooling around in the kelp. Still if your budding wreck hunter wishes to come up with the goods, then he or she must ignore the peer pressure, increase their research, keep the faith and continue to dive the site in the firm belief that eventually they will find something. Now on every dive I honestly believe that I will find something, anything from a fork to a porthole. On most dives of course you do not find anything, but at least you are 'tuned' in and ready to spot the slightest clue that could lead you finally to your wreck. If you think about it the law of averages are firmly on your side. If you put enough dives in then eventually you must find something, especially if your research is spot on. But you really must believe in your own ability or you will just give up and go home. A good example of this power of positive thinking is the wreck of the China tea clipper *Halloween* which struck the shore just inside the Hamstone on the edge of Soar Mill Cove on the evening of January 17, 1887.

The *Halloween* had the reputation for being one of the fastest ships of her day. On her maiden voyage in 1870 she took only sixty nine days to get to Sydney, and held the record for the fastest passage between London and Shanghi which she completed in a mere eighty nine days. The tea clippers represented the very pinnacle in sailing technology, and a major part of the *Halloween's* success lay in her seventy eight foot mainyard from which flew a huge mainsail. Iron hulled and sporting three masts laden with sails to catch every ounce of wind, the *Halloween* could cram sixteen hundred tons into her vast holds worth

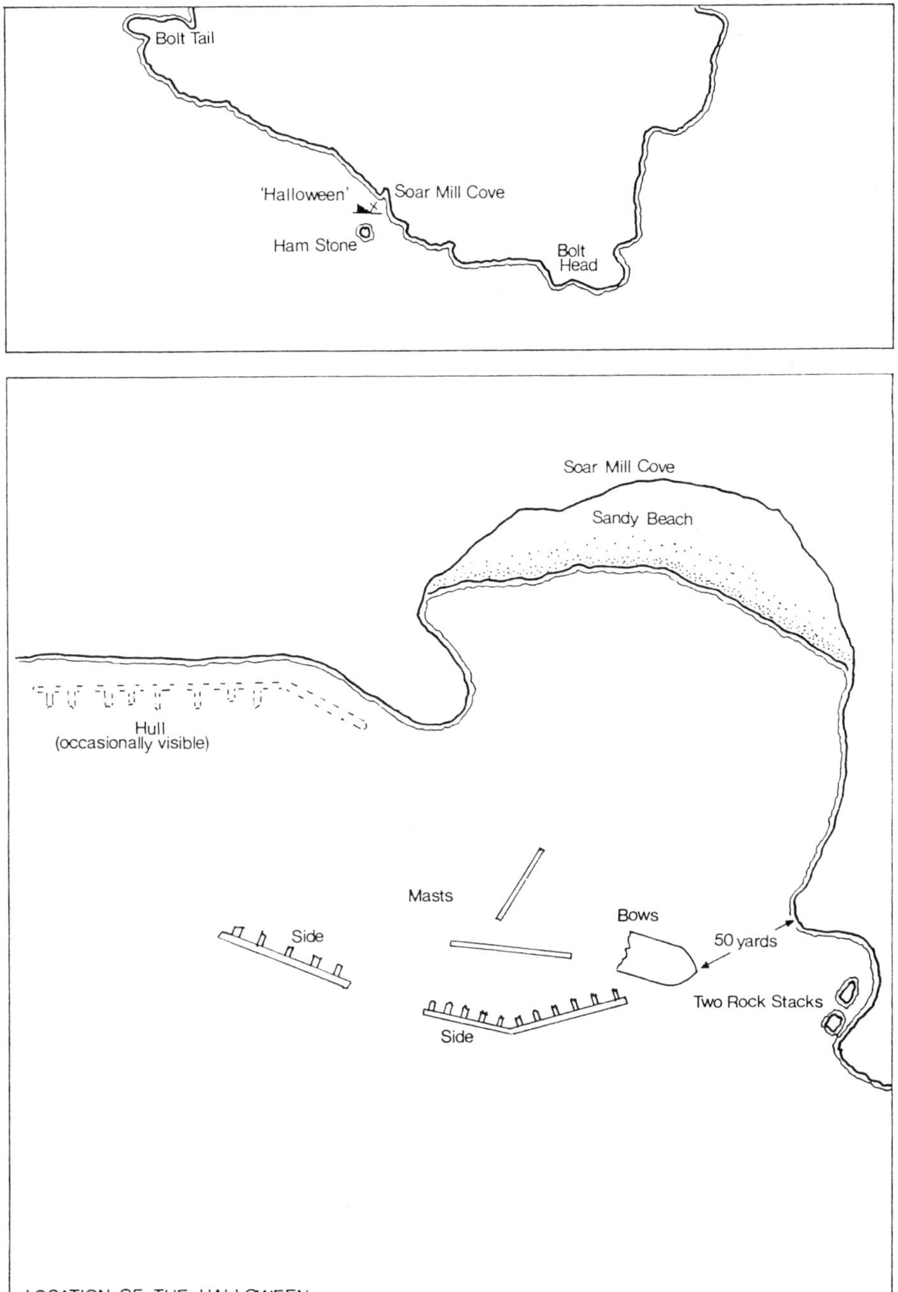

LOCATION OF THE HALLOWEEN

The *Herzogin Cecilie* aground in Soar Mill Cove almost exactly where the *Halloween* struck

Far right: Top, a porthole from the *Halloween*

Bottom: Marble from the *Volere* uncovered on the beach at Soar Mill Cove

well over forty thousand pound.

On what was to be her final voyage, she sailed from Foochow loaded with tea bound for London. But this time no records were to be broken. Right from the start bad weather slowed the *Halloween*, and it was to be one hundred and fifty five days before her exhausted crew finally saw the Eddystone Light square on her starboard side. A new course was set to safely take the ship some eight miles off Start Point. Running in huge seas, with the rain and wind beating relentlessly on the huge spread of sails, the *Halloween* somehow deviated from her set course, and in the howling darkness unsuspectingly drove in towards the shore. At half past seven in the evening the *Halloween* ran full tilt inside the west end of the Hamstone and crashed onto the rocks at the edge of Soar Mill Cove. She was

done for. In the heavy seas it was impossible for her to escape. The waves smashed the forecastle and cabin forcing the crew to take to the rigging until that too parted and they reluctantly returned to the deck. Flares were sent up, and even a bonfire built on the afterdeck, but nobody on shore took any notice. In the early morning three of the crew volunteered to try to take a line ashore. It was a desperate idea and unfortunately one of the brave volunteers was drowned in the attempt, but the other two managed to scramble ashore and stagger up the cliffs until they came to a farmhouse. More dead than alive they managed to stammer out their story to the farmer who quickly sent a message to Hope Cove, and the lifeboat was launched at about eight thirty. After a journey of almost an hour and a half the lifeboat managed to come alongside the *Halloween* and with some considerable difficulty extricated all nineteen crew who by this time were nearly frozen solid from their rigorous exposure to the bitterly cold conditions. Within three days the ship was broken up by repeated storms and her cargo of tea washed out of her broken hull and swept into Soar Mill Cove where it formed an almost impenetrable barrier some twelve feet high. Over the years the *Halloween* broke up and in time most of her was covered by about eight to ten feet of sand. The odd rusty plate and rib could be found close by the rocks but nothing much more. Slowly even they became covered by the sand and soon her passing became forgotten.

After researching this wreck Steve Carpenter and I were fairly sure that it was findable, and over about three years we dived in the area usually on the way back from other dives around Salcombe. In all that time we found absolutely nothing but still remained convinced that one day the wreck would surface. In February 1990 Steve took his dog for a walk at Soar Mill Cove. The tide was out and to his surprise so was most of the sand. What had been a beautiful sandy beach was now all rocks. Neither of us realised the significance of this until early May. Because of the storms, diving close to the shore in this area was useless due to the stirred up visibility. But as the high pressure systems settled down and the good weather continued I decided to chance it and go and take some photographs of the Cantabria. Conditions were good so on the way back I thought of having a snorkle in Soar Mill Cove, and cruised around in the boat. There was a small ground swell which made anchoring into just sand a bit difficult, but the water was nice and clear. Since the bottom was only about fifteen feet I looked for a clump of rocks to anchor into. Over to the right of the Cove I saw a dark shadow, and thinking it denoted rocks I threw my anchor in. When I was satisfied that the boat was well hooked, I assembled my camera gear and jumped in for a look around. Immediately I saw that I was hooked into a wreck. Right underneath me in twelve feet of water was a huge hatch, part of a bow, and a massive mast lying out across the sand. I just could not believe it. Steve and I, and the rest

the lines of the hull for instance just pushing up through the sand near the rocks to the left of the Cove. But as the year progressed no other major sections appeared more than a foot above the sand. Back in the main bow section, near the huge hatch, I later found two large anchors complete with some chain, and some large pulley blocks that were probably used to secure the boom. Steve, rooting in the sand by one of the masts pulled out a superb wooden Monkey block, and uncovered another large iron boom. As a dive in the long hot summer that we experienced that year it was magical, almost like being in the tropics. The fish although fairly small were many and varied, and even cuttle fish seemed content to play hide and seek around the wreckage without getting too frightened. Will any more of the *Halloween* appear, or will the storms shift the sand yet again and cover her for good? We shall have to wait and see. Whatever happens the *Halloween* justified my faith in positive thinking, and to see her after all those years is reward enough for me.

of my diving partners had dived this exact area on many occasions and found absolutely nothing. Now, at last, here was the wreck. At the bow (just like the photograph) you could see the remains of the once proud bowsprit, with wooden decking all around. As I ducked down again, I held on to the anchor rope to pull myself down. As I slowly turned to my left there, not twenty feet from my anchor lay a complete porthole glinting in the sunbeams. Now I knew what heaven was going to be like. Secured only by a few rusting bolts it came away easily, and when cleaned up revealed its makers name, J. Stone and Co. Deptford London. The rest of the day was really an anti climax, but as I drifted around the rest of the wreck I realised that there was almost no weed growth on any of the exposed wreckage. This meant that it had only been uncovered for a few days at most. (We took some photo's for comparison a month later and the wreck was almost obscured by weed.) I had been incredibly lucky. Over the next few weeks different sections of the wreck started to appear,

See if you can spot the anchor

One of the main masts of the *Halloween*

Far right: 'The Duchess'

CHAPTER 8

THE WRECK OF THE ARMED MERCHANT STEAMER RIVERSDALE

BOLT TAIL TO PRAWLE POINT

The advent of the First World War saw many new innovations, the most profound being the advance of the aeroplane, from something of a music hall joke to a serious fighting machine. The military were not slow to see its advantages and for a time its development overshadowed other even more warlike machines. One such was the evolution of the submarine. The British, with characteristic stupidity, had condemned underwater warfare as tantamount to cold blooded murder, and definately not sporting. The Germans however knew a winner when they saw it, and churned out hundreds of the deadly craft and soon were gaily sinking thousands of tons of British shipping while the Navy, who had never had any qualms about undersea warfare, murder or not, pointed the finger at the politicians. In the meantime the U boats had it all their own way, and in an age before the wolf packs had been invented they sectioned off their killing grounds into huge boxes so that each submarine had a set target area. One of the best was the box that encompassed both the Eddystone and Start Point. Nearly every ship that passed up the Channel had to come through this box, and on the night of December 18 1917 the armed British merchant steamer *Riversdale* was to be no exception.

Built in 1906 by J. Blumer & Co. of Sunderland, the *Riversdale* was 317 feet long with a gross tonnage of some 2805 tons, and was en route from the Tyne to Savona in Italy loaded with a cargo of coal. Lurking in her path was the German submarine U.B. 31 commanded by Oberleutnant Bieber. As the *Riversdale* came abeam of the Start Light Bieber picked up the noise of her single screw and rose to periscope depth to have a look. There in the pale moonlight he could see the cargo vessel plainly silhouetted, steaming slowly towards him. As the *Riversdale* came within range, Bieber loosed a torpedo which struck the vessel, causing such an explosion that Bieber, confident the *Riversdale* would sink called off the attack and hightailed it north east towards Dartmouth where he caught up with another collier, the Alice Marine, and sent her to the bottom.

Meanwhile the *Riversdale* had surprised herself and her crew by staying afloat and her skipper, Capt. Simpson, was now battling to get her safely to the shore. In this he succeeded, finally running her aground near Prawle Point. Luckily the weather was in his favour, and apart from one crewman lost in the initial explosion, all the rest of the crew were saved. Salvage experts quickly arrived on the scene and soon decided that with a bit of effort the *Riversdale* could be saved. To this end bulkheads were shored up and compressors were installed to get rid of the water and keep a check on leaks from the patch that had been hastily cobbled together around the torpedo hole. Tugs were sent for, towing arrangements made, and with a mounting sense

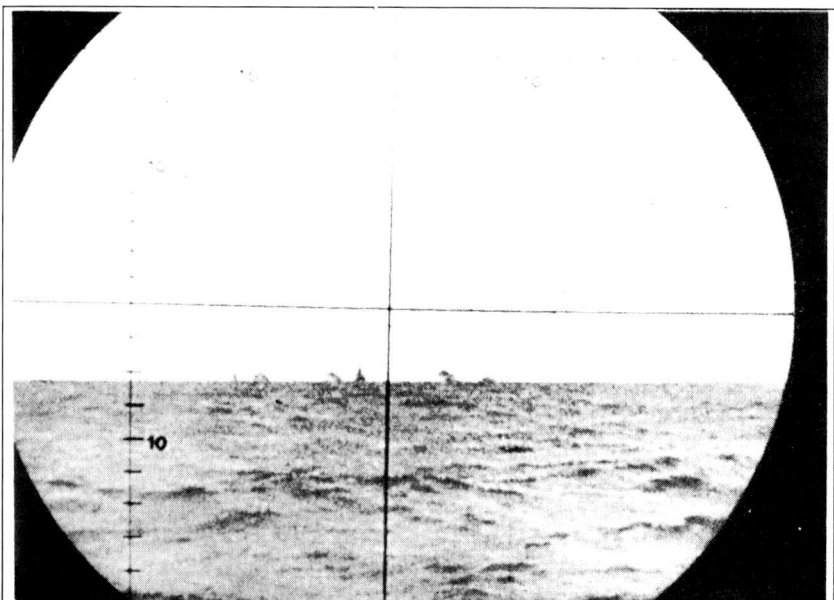

U Boat periscope view of a merchant convoy

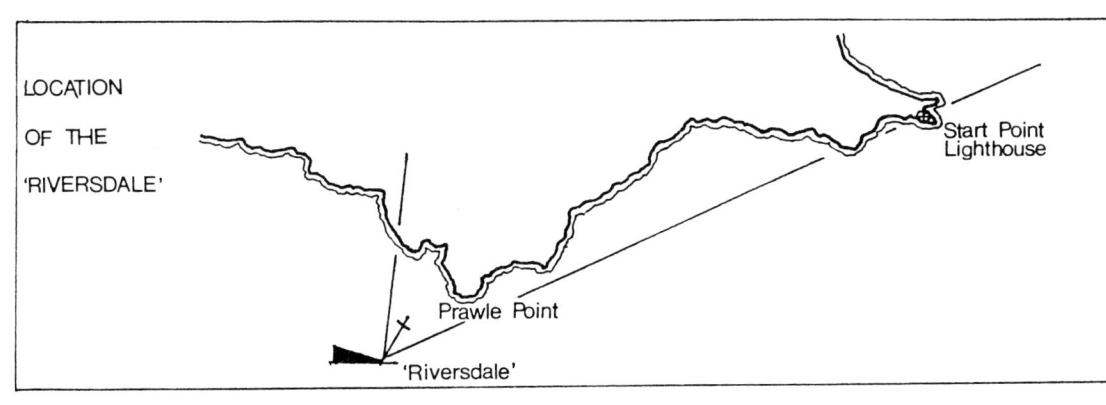

LOCATION
OF THE
'RIVERSDALE'

Start Point
Lighthouse

Prawle Point

'Riversdale'

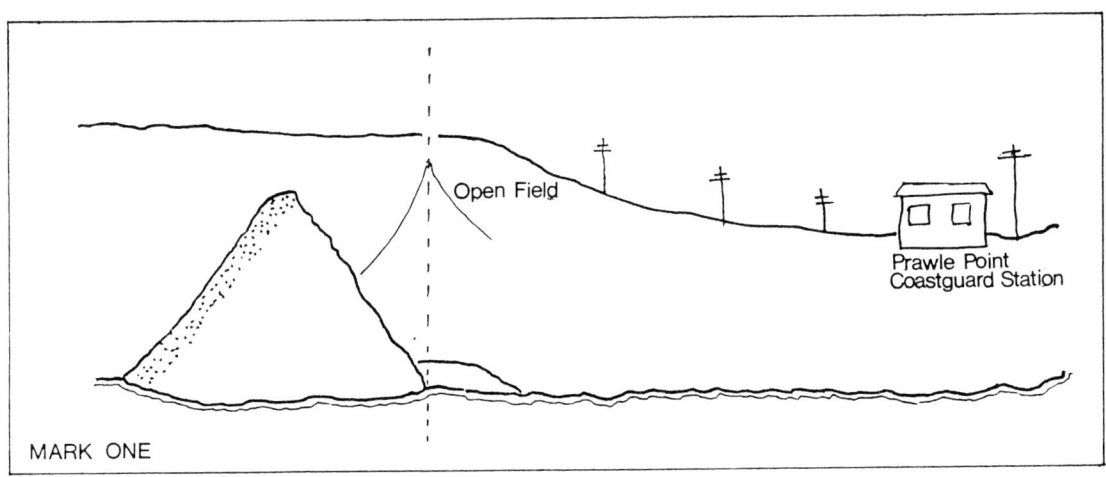

Open Field

Prawle Point
Coastguard Station

MARK ONE

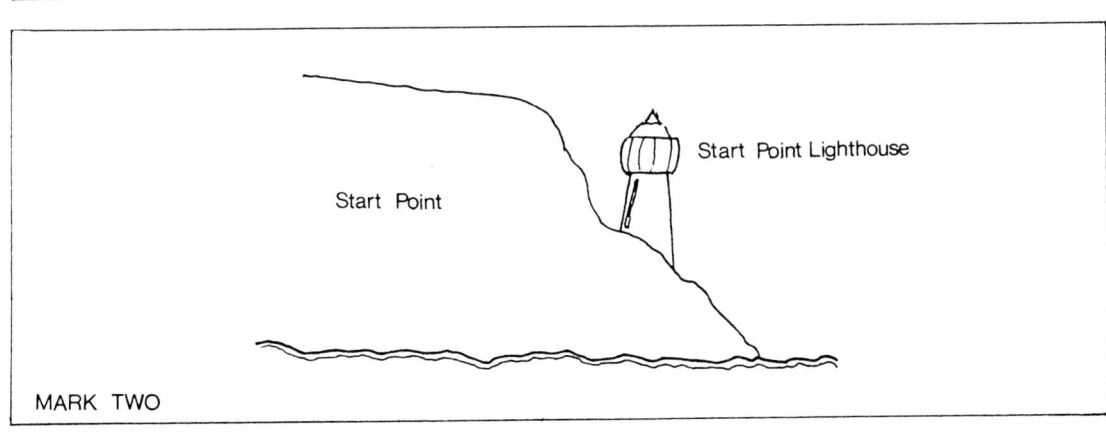

Start Point Lighthouse

Start Point

MARK TWO

of confidence the *Riversdale* was pulled off the rocky shore. She came off without too much trouble, but before the vessel had gone more than a thousand yards the patch blew off and the *Riversdale* gently sank, nice and upright in about 42 metres of water. As she hit the bottom her bow broke away and in later years her superstructure was wire swept and dispersed.

Even with all the wire sweeping this wreck still sits up 45 feet or so from the sea bed and so is quite easy to find once you have sorted out where the marks for the marks are. This bit of coast is rather bland, so study the markss carefully and then confirm with your echo sounder. If you are hooked, then you are on it because there is nothing else in the area and the sea bed is just sand. The visibility on the *Riversdale* is usually very good, 20 to 30 feet being the norm, and because it is in a relatively sheltered area it can be dived on most occasions. However the tidal streams in this area are very strong, so slack water is by far the best time to dive her. Once on the wreck you will find that in some ways it is very remininiscent of the James Egan Layne a few years ago. The wreck is virtually still intact and has massive holds that you can swim into just like the Egan Layne. Since it is a good bit deeper however, it is not as light inside the holds and your exit points are limited, so distance reels are very necessary. At the stern the wreck still has its great iron propellor supported by huge brackets, and it is here that you probably get the best indication of her size as you swim from the deck, down over the stern to the prop and the sand below. Scattered around the wreck is part of its cargo of coal, and local divers quite often raise some in sacks for their own use. A nice bonus this, I always think, as this type of coal always seems to burn with a weird green and blue flame. Smashing on a dark cold night.

The fish life on this wreck is not as prolific as others in the area, maybe because it is heavily fished by anglers. Once again there are a lot of old lines hanging around, so make sure that your knife is sharp. All in all the *Riversdale* is one of my favourite 'deep' wrecks because it is easy to find, nice and intact, and has that feel about it that makes you think you are going to find something really nice. To date no such luck. But one day, who knows?

Far left: This piece
would not come off

Above left: Peering into
a hatch on the *Riversdale*

Above right: Inside a
hold on the *Riversdale*

81

S. S. SOUDAN

Right name, right size, but I am not convinced that it is the right ship

THE WRECK OF THE SOUDAN

In the early morning of the 27 June 1887 the Hamstone was shrouded in dense fog. Creeping up the Channel towards Dunkirk was the 844 ton French steamer *Soudan*, loaded with peanuts, ox hides, and oil from Senegal. The eight passengers and twenty four crew, now only hours from a safe landfall gazed worriedly out at the eerie, swirling fog and prayed that the Captain knew where he was. Unfortunately their prayers went unanswered because shortly before mid day the *Soudan* ran straight out of the fog onto the Hamstone where she became firmly stuck. Still with a flat calm sea the only casualty was the Captain's pride. When the fog lifted that afternoon the eight passengers were rescued by a passing yatch, which took them to Salcombe where they reported the *Soudan* firmly stuck on the outer ledges of the Hamstone, with about twelve feet of water in her forward holds. By that

evening the tugs Vixen and Raleigh had arrived on the scene, and as the tide rose the *Soudan* floated free of the Hamstone enabling the two tugs to take her in tow.

Although the crew had sealed off the forward holds the water was still leaking into the vessel in considerable quantities, and the *Soudan* became very sluggish and difficult to manoeuvre. Progress was desperately slow. By midnight the tugs had managed to tow the *Soudan* abreast the Mewstones and started to make the turn for the entrance to Salcombe Harbour. With water still pouring into the forward holds past the sealed bulkheads, the stress on the other bulkheads increased. In the end the engine room bulkhead gave way with a loud tearing noise and the tug skippers suddenly realised that they were now towing a dead weight that had to power to take them both to the bottom. Hurriedly they rushed

82

to cut the towing hawsers now humming ominously with the strain. The *Soudan* seemed to catapult forward then dived bows under the waves to come to rest upright on the bottom with her mast still visible above the surface.

By the time morning came the *Soudan's* cargo had started to float out of her, but the insurers were optimistic, especially as she seemed to still be more of less in one piece. Two Belgium salvage ships, the Berger Wilhelm and the Newa, were hired to raise the wreck, and for two months they stayed on site trying every trick in the book. Air was blown into her ballast tanks, and when that failed huge air bags were placed into her holds and compressors pumped air down to them for days. Nothing happened. Next, massive chains were passed underneath her hull and secured to lifting lighters, which besides using powerful winches also used the lifting effects of the tides. But all was to no avail, the *Soudan* seemed determined to stay on the bottom. After a few more abortive attempts the owners and insurers gave up in despair and declared the *Soudan* a complete and total loss.

Today the *Soudan* lies in exactly the same place in about 60 feet of water on a sandy bottom. Although broken up her stern is still reasonably intact as are her boilers. An interesting feature of this wreck is her iron propellor with its well polished boss, a tribute to the many divers that visit her. The bows stand out of the sand with the foredeck and some bulkheads lying flat on the sea bed with what appears to be part of the mainmast and boom lying across all of that. The boom leads you out onto the sand where other pieces of bulkhead and ribs lie scattered. It is an easy and compact wreck to swim around and the boilers serve as a nice central point from which to get your bearings. Even though this wreck is very popular with visiting divers there are still

A pipe fitting on one of the boilers from the *Soudan*

83

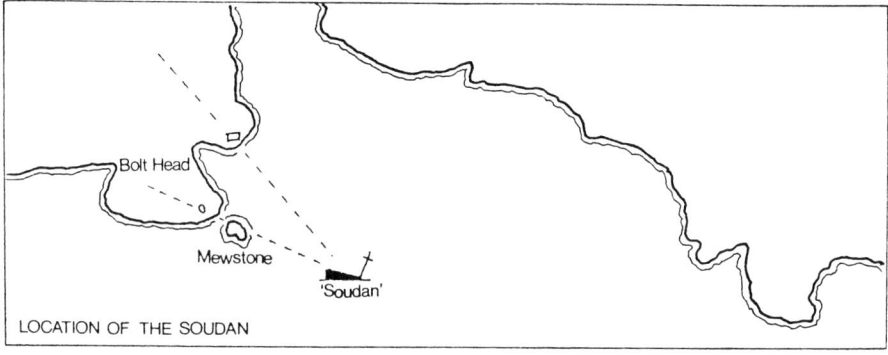

LOCATION OF THE SOUDAN

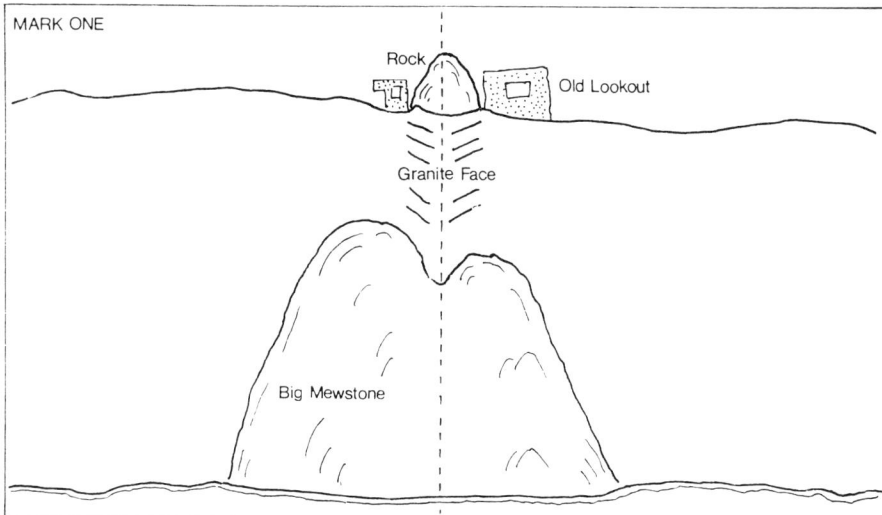

MARK ONE

Rock

Old Lookout

Granite Face

Big Mewstone

small brass valves and tally's to be found and occasionally the odd china door knob turns up.

Because of her position the *Soudan* is only divable for twenty minutes of slack water at both high and low tide. Even this is a bit variable and when the tide starts running it really shifts so strick timekeeping and good boat cover are essential. The tide run also makes the visibility somewhat unpredictable. Usually it is about fifteen feet, but sometimes the tide just deposits all the rubbish from the estuary on the wreck site and the visibility can drop to very disappointing levels. If you aim to dive in the middle of summer the boat traffic in and out of Salcombe Harbour is reminiscent of the Chiswick Flyover in the bad old days, so make sure that you have a large 'A' flag. In spite of all this do not be put off. The *Soudan* is well worth diving, but because of the time factor a series of dives will be much more rewarding than just a single one.

Incidentally, the photo of the *Soudan* is not to be taken as gospel. It is the right size, right shape, and it has the right name, but I have worries about the date. Extensive research has not come up with anything better but I am still not convinced that this is the right *Soudan*. I offer it more as a good illustration of what the *Soudan* probably looked like in the hope that it will add some enjoyment to your diving.

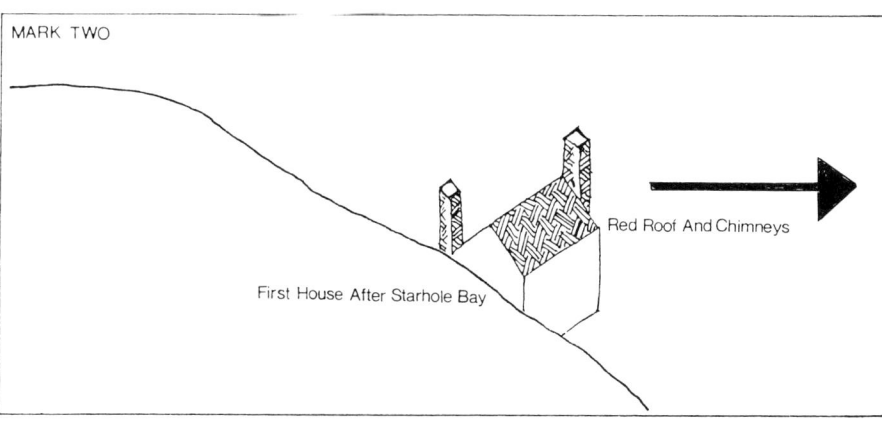

MARK TWO

Red Roof And Chimneys

First House After Starhole Bay

THE WRECK OF THE HERZOGIN CECILIE

Above: Unloading some of the grain from 'The Duchess'

Right: Towing 'The Duchess' to Starhole Bay

Previous page: The *Herzogin Cecilie* aground in Soar Mill Cove

When I was a child some of my favourite stories were about the great Australian grain races, and the Tea Clippers sailing across the oceans from China. The photographs and drawings of those huge sailing ships fascinated me, and no doubt countless others, because today, 'Tall Ships' as they are now called, draw enthusiastic crowds in much the same way that steam trains do. People nowadays put this crowd pulling down to nostalgia, but even in their heyday these massive sailing ships with their graceful lines and billowing sails drew even bigger crowds, and many had songs and stories woven around their legendary voyages.

Probably the very last of these ships to be wrecked on the south coast of England was the *Herzogin Cecilie*, or as she was more affectionally known, the *Duchess*. She was a four masted steel barque built by Rickmers of Bremerhaven in 1902 as a school ship for the North German Lloyd Line, and was 314 feet long with a gross tonnage of 3242 tons. When the Great War started the *Herzogin Cecilie* was interned in Chile for the duration, and afterwards she was allocated to France by the War Reparations Board. The Germans tried to repurchase her but were turned down flat, and eventually she passed into Finnish ownership, being bought and commanded by Captain Gustaf Erickson of Mariehamn. Under his ownership the *Herzogin Cecilie* carried cargoes all over the world, but it was the Australian Grain Races that made her famous, winning eight of them in succession.

In 1936 the *'Duchess'* started what was to be her last voyage and her last Grain Race. From

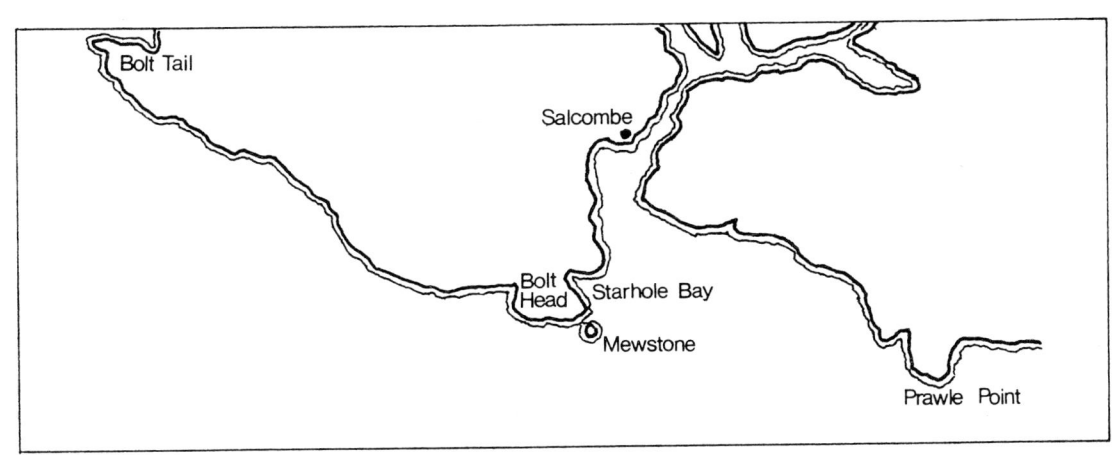

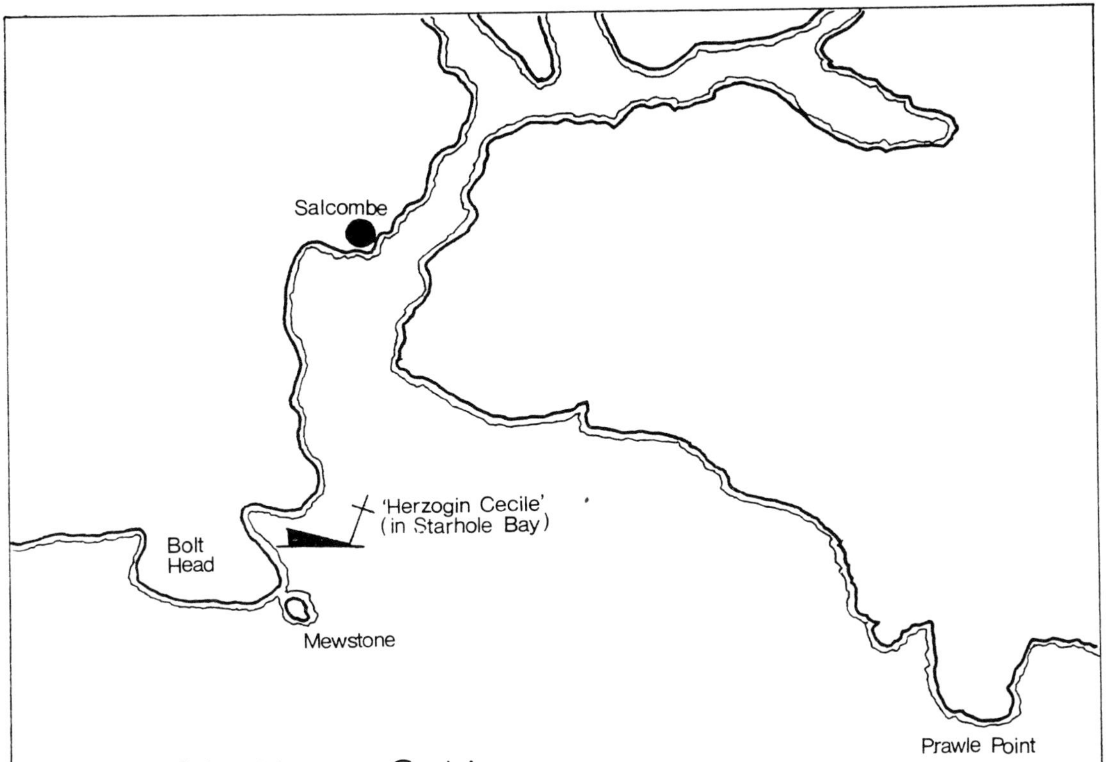

Bolt Tail

Salcombe

Bolt
Head

Starhole Bay

Mewstone

Prawle Point

Salcombe

Bolt
Head

'Herzogin Cecile'
(in Starhole Bay)

Mewstone

Prawle Point

Location of the 'Herzogin Cecile'

Port Lincon in Australia to Falmouth took her just 86 days, comfortably beating her nearest rival, the Pommern, by seven whole days. Her orders at Falmouth were to proceed to Ipswich to discharge her cargo of grain, but two days later, early on the morning of the 25 January, in thick fog and rough seas the *Herzogin Cecilie* struck the Hamstone just a few miles from Salcombe. Holed in the forepeak, the ship pounded fiercely, then settled by her head with her well decks awash. When dawn broke just about everybody and his aunt had turned up to view the wreck, and quite a lot thought that they should also go on board. This considerably

A resident of the wreck site.

hampered the rescue operations, but in the end the Salcombe lifeboat took off twenty two of the crew, leaving just the Captain, his wife, and six crew members. A breeches buoy was rigged up to take off all the luggage and personal belongings, but most of this was quickly stolen when it landed by members of the public, who had by now degenerated into something of a mob.

For seven weeks the *Herzogin Cecilie* lay stranded on the Hamstone whilst her four and a half thousand tons of grain rotted and fermented. The stench was appaulling and fears of it polluting the beaches around Salcombe kept the owner and the local council arguing fit to bust. Every day huge crowds gathered to view the '*Duchess*' and local farmers made a fortune charging people to cross their land for a better look. Eventually the grain became so swollen that it started to crack the decks, and this seemed to galvanise the salvage attempts. By June 7 enough of her rotting cargo had been removed to allow the installation of powerful pumps, and on each high tide tugs repeatedly attempted to pull her off. At first it looked as if the '*Duchess*' was stuck fast, but finally, on 19 June the *Herzogin Cecilie* floated clear of the Hamstone. The local council still would not let her be towed into Salcombe, fearing all manner of disease, so in the end the '*Duchess*' was beached in Starhole Bay just at the entrance to the harbour. Unfortunately what appeared to be a 'safe' sandy bottom, concealed rocks, and in the July gales she broke her back and her masts soon tumbled down into the sea. It was the beginning of the end. Ironically, if the Salcombe authorities had allowed her into harbour she would have been saved, unloaded and on her way long before the gales came. As it was the thing that the council feared most happened. The grain washed out of the wreck and fetched up on all the beaches. However it didn't cause any pollution because the seagulls ate most of it, and the rest got washed away. So much for the experts.

In the ensuing months all the fittings were stripped from the wreck, the beautiful figurehead sent to a museum in Finland, and the remains sold to a local scrap merchant for the princely sum of £225. A sorry end for a marvellous ship.

Inside the bows of the *Herzogin Cecilie*

Today at low tide, the remains of the *'Duchess'* just about show. In the summer there is always a buoy attached to the wreck, (at the bows) and it is prominently marked on all the charts, so you really cannot miss it. Still if you do, just ask, everybody knows about her, and most will be glad to point her out. The wreckage lies in less than 25 feet of water on a sandy bottom, and I had been told that there was just a jumble of iron plates, and that the wreck was hardly worth diving on. Not so. The *Herzogin Cecilie* must be one of the prettiest wreck sites going. Part of the bows is angled over to form a sort of cave into which you can easily swim to play with the many wrasse that lurk there. Stray light twinkles in from various small jagged holes backlighting the interior with a soft glow. Marvellous for underwater photography. There is a huge amount of iron plating and decking lying across the sand and also pushed into the sand. There is quite a lot of material from which the sails were made buried in the sand, but what I really like about this wreck are the tunnels. Various parts of the deck and hull have fallen down in such a way as to make iron tunnels along the sand. They are not really that long, and you can usually see to the end, but they are a bit special. In the tunnels, the seaweed catches the light and the current as it wafts in and out of the ragged openings, along with a myriad of small fish. It really is most enjoyable, and on one dive we all spent at least twenty minutes just swimming in and out of these tunnels. The rest of the wreck stretches out along the bay, and it is still possible to find wooden decking, and the iron pulleys that once held the ropes that hoisted up the great sails.

It's a great jigsaw of a wreck, and you can either put it together, or just poke and prod about. The *Herzogin Cecilie* will always be remembered as one of the great square riggers, but it is as a wreck that she really lives up to her old nick name, the *'Duchess'* a real charmer.

THE BRONZE AGE WRECK

Ships over 300 years old are very rarely found, but when they are they often provide unique glimpses into how people lived in those far off days. Often the way the ships themselves were constructed is fairly well documented but the marine archeologists are always eager to confirm their theories, and anyway it is always fascinating to see the way the old shipwrights put these ships together. However if you go back past the time of the Vikings old shipwrecks in our part of the world are decidedly thin on the ground, and if we travel back in time 3000 years then no ancient shipwreck of this period has so far been discovered in all of Northern Europe. Now we know that men sailed across the English Channel in prehistoric times and that means that they must have been able to build fairly sturdy craft. However very little is known about these craft or what they were like. Certainly by the third millenium B.C. boats made by hollowing out tree trunks were being used in Northern Europe, and on the Humber Estuary three boats constructed of sawn planks were discovered and were thought to have been used in the second millenium. These however were fairly insubstantial craft and not really suited to open water voyaging.

From what historians have pieced together it probably just was not worth anybody building substantial ships because the amount of load carrying for trading purposes just was not needed. Not needed that it until the dawn of the Bronze Age. By about 1500 B.C. bronze tools were becoming plentiful and as demand for them increased the early shipbuilders gained the necessary expertise required to build ships capable of sustained open water voyaging. They had to because only seaworthy ships could transport copper and tin, the essential ingredients of bronze, to those places cut off by the sea. If you look out over the English Channel it is fairly obvious that most of the trading would have been concentrated at the narrowest part. Bronze age settlements around what we now know as Dover seem fairly certain, and so it was not too surprising when in 1974 members of a local sub aqua club came across bronze objects in the chalk gullies at Langdon Bay just up from Dover Harbour. After finding nearly a hundred pieces the club took them to a local museum where they were identified as tools and weapons from bronze age France. The bronzes went to the British museum, the divers were patted on the head and went off to discover many more artefacts. But the academics just filed it away much to the chagrin of later archeologists.

In July 1977 a diving instructor called Philip Baker was instructing a beginner, John Clarks in shallow water off the Pigs Nose at Moor Sands about halfway between Salcombe and Prawle Point. In 23 feet of water on a patch of sand he found a bronze age sword with a hook tang. About an hour later Clarks found an eroded bronze blade not far from where the first had been found. Now it was very lucky that Baker had an interest in old Naval swords or he probably would not have realised how important his find was. As a collector he knew that he had got hold of something out of the ordinary and he set off to find an expert. The expert turned out to be the well known underwater archeologist Keith Muckelroy, and by September he and Baker had had their first preliminary recognisance which turned up another worn and battered bronze blade. Three blade in one fairly small area led Muckelroy to the tentative conclusion that they had probably come from a bronze age shipwreck. He decided to launch a full survey and on his recommendation the Moor Sand site was designated under the Protection of Wrecks Act.

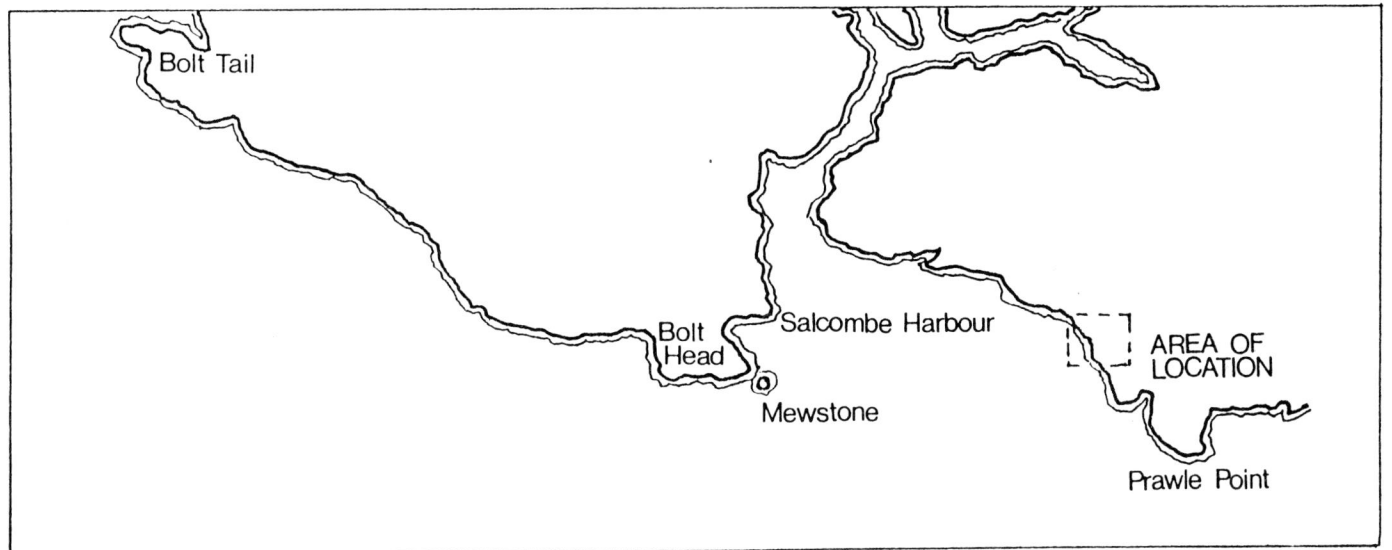

Moor Sand posed Muckelroy and his team of divers quite severe logistical problems because of the absence of any roads down to the site. Nearly all the equipment had to be shipped in and after establishing a wooden hut well above the high water mark as a base camp, he had an aerial flightway constructed to shift equipment from the hut to the beach. Muckelroy's first task was to systematically search the area of sea bed around the place where the original blades had been found. Firstly this would place them in their context on the sea bed, and would then allow him to see if any more bronze age artefacts could be found close by. It was fairly obvious that when Baker found his first sword it had recently been disturbed by tidal movement as it could not have possibly lain undamaged for any length of time on such a severely scoured sea bed.

The divers started searching through the sand and thick kelp in corridors measuring 100 metres by 10 metres. Starting from opposite sides of the corridor a pair of divers would swim slowly towards each other, searching the sea bed until they met up. On the exposed patches of sand or shingle the divers would gently fan the area with their hands to see if anything was buried just below the surface. It was a painstaking business.

Later their searches were backed up by metal detectors, but the going was very slow. Often it took two days to complete a full search of just one corridor. In all that year the divers searched a total of about four acres of sea bed and it took them four weeks before they came up with their first find, a palstave, a type of axe head, lying completely exposed on a bit of bare rock. By the end of the season they had found a companion axe head and one more corroded sword blade.

In 1979, after a very bad winter the search was resumed, this time going further afield, (see diagram) but significantly the only find of note was a large bronze blade much larger than the original ones, possibly the remains of a much larger sword or even some type of rapier. The fact that it was found right in the middle of the previous years' search area caused the archeologists to put on their thinking caps, but no proper explanation could be found except for the bad winter possibly stirring things up. Most of the blades were consistent with artefacts found in the Seine Basin and Eastern France, whilst the palstaves were both of a type known to have been manufactured in Northwest France. So what have we got? The geologists considered that recent substantial cliff erosion was unlikely,

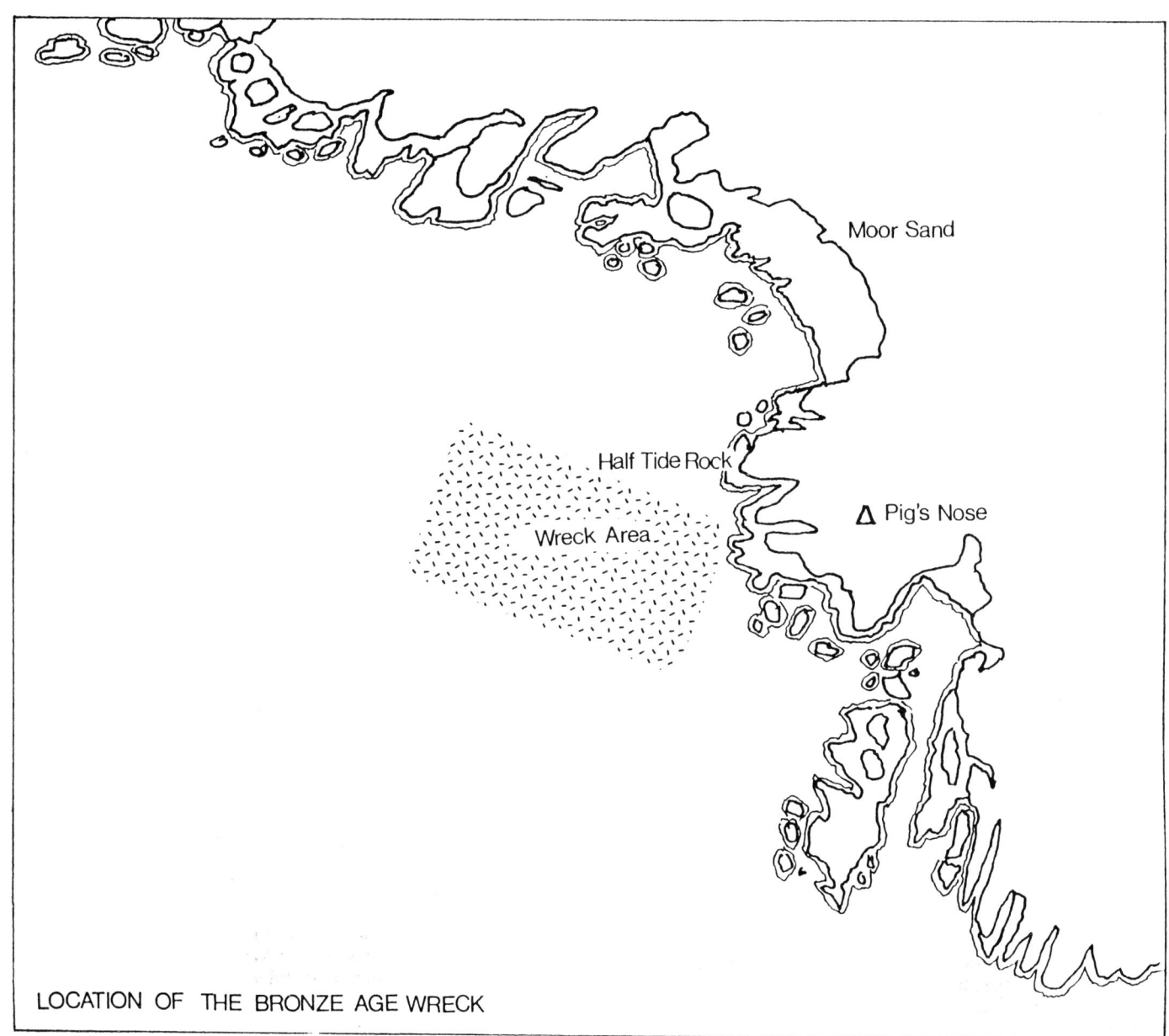

Moor Sand

Half Tide Rock

△ Pig's Nose

Wreck Area

LOCATION OF THE BRONZE AGE WRECK

which meant that probably the bronze artefacts had not come from any land deposit. So the archeologists were left with the argument that all the artefacts came across from France in one ship which was then wrecked. It is a bit tenuous and the evidence is inconclusive to say the least. The site is still protected and occasionally new searches are carried out, but so far with no results.

Still there were quite extensive networks of trade across the Channel back in the bronze age, and Prawle Point and Bolt Tail are good land marks. If you think about the Halloween buried all those years underneath the sand, who knows? If the bronze age sailors came over here they would have done what sailors down through the ages have done. They would have wrecked some of their ships somewhere along this part of the coast. So it is not too improbable to hope that somewhere underneath the sand and shingle off Moor Sands lie the remains of a bronze age ship.

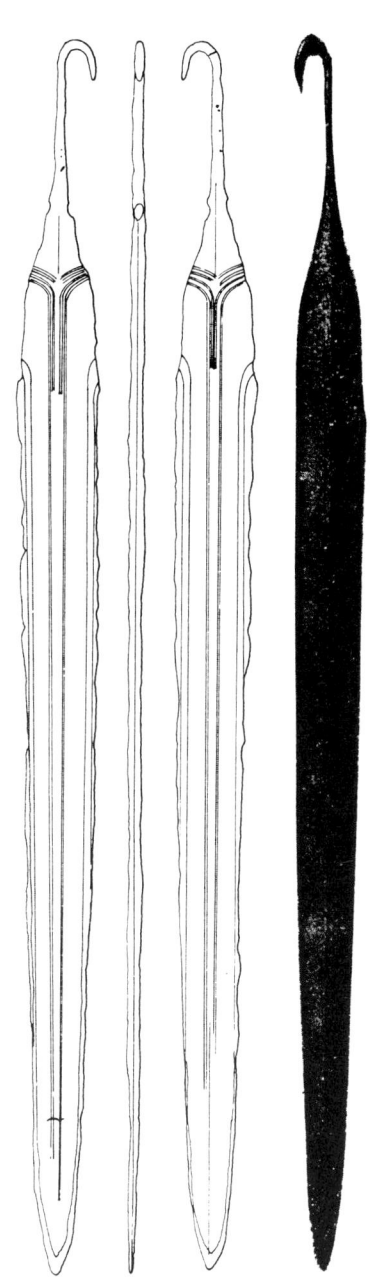

Bronze age swords with hook tangs

Ascending in a cloud of bubbles

CHAPTER 9

PRAWLE POINT ... SHIP TRAP ...

The *Louis Yvonne*

WESTCOUNTRY COUNCIL ELECTIONS

Labour Activity At Exeter

WHERE FIGHTS ARE PROBABLE

Interesting Position At Torquay

TWO VESSELS ON ROCKS

Victims Of Dense Channel Fog

FRENCH COASTER AT PRAWLE POINT

6,000 Tons Steamer's Plight At Lizard

French vessel Louis Yvonne ran on to the rocks at Prawle during Thursday night's fog. Picture shows there can be little hope of successful salvage.

DEVON COUNTY SHOW EPILOGUE

Thanks And Gifts To Barnstaple Officials

MAYOR AND FARMERS

HARBOUR TO BE SOLD

Paignton Council Offer £7,500

PHEASANT SEASON PROSPECTS

Detrimental Frosts

WESTCOUNTRY BIRDS BELOW NORMAL

Introduction

I have sometimes heard it said that if you could pull out the plug from the bottom of the sea, you could almost walk from Plymouth to Start Point over the remains of all the ships that have been wrecked along this part of the South Devon coast. To some this might seem an exaggeration until you realise that in 1804 on one day alone in Deadmans Bay, just yards from Plymouth's famous Barbican, ten ships were driven ashore during fierce southerly gales. That kind of tally was by no means exceptional, and before Plymouth built its great breakwater the port was fast becoming known as the graveyard of the British Navy. But, bad as it was, probably the most notorious stretch of water along this trecherous coastline was, and still is the six miles between Bolt Tail and Start Point, and only God knows just how many men have died, and how many ships have been smashed to pieces on its unforgiving shore. In one horrific incident near Bolt Tail in 1760, the Ramillies, a 90 gun ship of the line was swept into the cave that now bears her name, and in a few short minutes was pounded to tiny fragments. Over seven hundred people died trying to scramble out of the raging seas and up the sheer cliffs to safety.

What is extraordinary however, is not so much the disaster aspect of the wrecks, (if you have ever been off this part of the coast in a storm you will quickly appreciate that any mistakes are almost bound to lead to catastrophe) but the way certain areas seem to act as magnets for stricken vessels. The Hamstone, midway between Bolt Tail and Bolt Head for example collected three clipper ships and at least two steamers in just fifty years, and we will never know how many hit the surrounding area in vain efforts to take avoiding action. But the one area along this coast that seems to be outstanding in its ability to act as a ship trap, is *Prawle Point*.

On a sunny day this is the perfect spot for a picnic. The smooth sea gently laps around a rocky point, almost forming an island, and the

"Ida" ashore in fog at Prawle Point Sept. 1930.

The Ida aground just off the 'Island'

cliffs gentle out to small slopes allowing easy access to the rock strewn beach. But come the storms all this calm is swept away with high waves breaking over the point and rushing savagely between the island and the shore creating a maelstrom of turbulent water and driving spray. Whilst many ships have struck the outside of *Prawle Point*, a significant number have managed to end up caught in between the jaws of the island and the mainland's shore, and that's where the real ship trap lies. Most never escape, but in 1926 the Dutch steamer *Betsy Anna* had a stroke of good luck and proved to be a rare exception. She had stranded in thick fog on the morning of 17 August and ended wedged straight up between the island and the mainland. The weather however was very calm, and by the 3 October the *Betsy Anna* was towed of by the tug Trustee and beached near Salcombe for repairs. Nine days later she was towed towards Cowes, but as she was rounding Portland Bill her luck ran out, her tow parted and down she went.

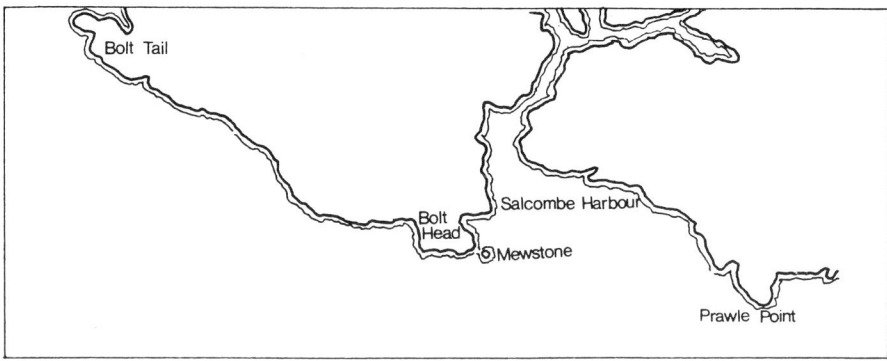

PRAWLE POINT ...

In more recent times *Prawle Point* has enticed three more ships into its island trap, and they unfortunately did not escape. Today their remains lie inextricably linked together, where storms and tide have gathered them. Because of this tangle of wreckage I am going to deal with all three wrecks together, because when you dive here you will be swimming over all three wrecks and will have great difficulty telling one from another. If I take the wrecks in chronological order of sinking, we begin with the seamer *Ida*. She was on passage from Cardiff to Portsmouth with a cargo of coal. Approaching *Prawle Point* in thick fog, she safely weathered the Mewstones off Bolt Head, but did not alter course enough to miss the *Prawle*. At about four o'clock on 22 September 1930 she struck the two rocks that show at half tide just in front of the entrance to the small channel that runs inside *Prawle Point* and the 'island', and jammed hard aground. Luckily for the crew of twelve the coastguard rescued all of them in double quick time, and soon all were happily warming themselves in the local pub. At first it was hoped that the *Ida* would be refloated and some of her coal was removed to help lighten the load. But all to no avail. The *Ida* remained stuck fast on the rocks until early October when a gale broke her back, and subsequent storms smashed her to pieces. The *Ida* had to wait five long years before she had company.

On the morning of 29 September 1935 the French vessel *Louis Yvonne* was outward bound from Penzance to Torquay with a cargo of onions, when she ran aground in dense fog in precisely the same place as the *Betsy Anna* nine years earlier. The crew of four and two women managed to jump off the boat onto the rocks, and safely made their way in the fog up to the nearby village. Come the dawn it was obvious that the boat was too well jammed to get her off and it was found that the bottom had been badly stove in when she grounded. The *Louis Yvonne* broke up over the next few months, and until fairly recently her bows could still be seen at low tide. This state of affairs changed in 1979

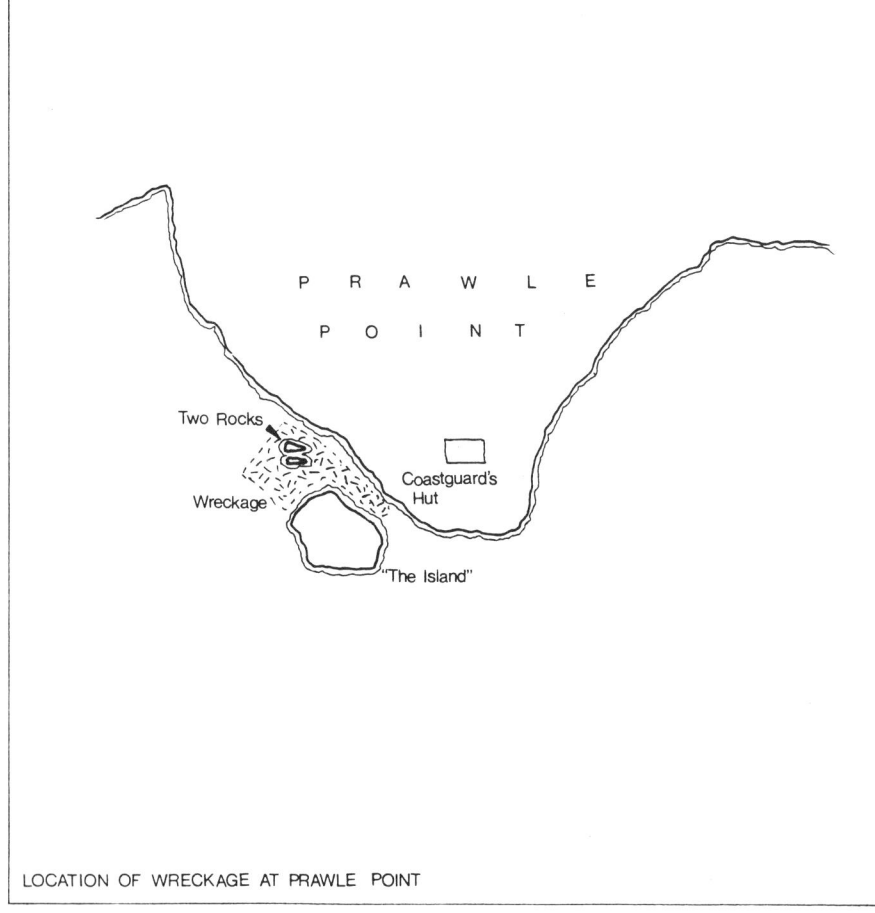

LOCATION OF WRECKAGE AT PRAWLE POINT

when the 420 ton coaster *Heye-P* was overwhelmed by hurrican force winds on her way from Par in Cornwall to Velsen, West Germany, loaded with china clay. Drifting helplessly out of control, the *Heye-P* was pushed relentlessly towards *Prawle Point*. As huge waves broke over the ship, the crew began to realise that if the vessel struck the shore they would probably all perish. Suddenly out of the darkness came two bright beams of light from search lights set up on the shore by the coastguards. With their aid a rescue helicopter, its pilot nearly blinded by the huge sheets of spray whipped up by the gale force winds, managed to hover over the ship's deck long enough to winch all three crew to safety. Minutes after the last man was plucked from the deck the ship struck the rocks with such force that she immediately broke her back, and very quickly became a total loss.

Today the remains of the *Heye-P* and the *Louis Yvonne* are easy to find because they both came to grief directly underneath the coastguard station. Parts of the bow of the *Heye-P* were easily visible even above the high water mark, but recent storms have smashed them up and swept parts of them out towards where the remains of the *Ida* lie. Even so at low water part of the stern of the *Heye-P* becomes visible and the rest of the wreckage is impossible to miss. The only trouble is, which wreck is which.

If you swim up inside the gorge that separates the 'island' and the mainland, you will find the remains of both the *Louis Yvonne* and the *Heye-P*'s bows. When it was wrecked, the *Heye-P* actually came to rest right on top of the *Louis Yvonne*, with its bows sticking right up in the

The *Heye-P* smashed onto Prawle Point

97

air. Now they both lie in about thirty feet of water on a very rocky bottom. The tide rip through the gorge is very, very strong and makes safe diving here only possible at slack water. Looking out from the gorge the two rocks where the *Ida* ran aground are easy to spot and that is where most of the wreckage has collected. However around the stern section of the *Heye-P* there is a lot of broken wreckage, with the debris of iron railings, cable drums, hatch covers, old fire extinguishers, and the remains of winches littering the whole area. In between the two rocks you will find part of another bow, probably the *Ida's*, together with a large anchor, part of a boiler, and what looks like a propellor shaft. Further over towards the 'island' is a huge section of hull from the *Heye-P* lying wedged between a jumble of large rocks.

As you swim around the rocks away from the shore the kelp starts to be a problem, but most of the large sections are lying in the sandy bits in between. Even so the bottom is still very rocky with large boulders that can cause problems if you are thrown unexpectedly upon them. Because of the strong tidal streams in this area the ground swell can be very irritating, even on what seems to be a calm day, and can also cause the visibility to drop quite dramatically.

Incidentally do not be too surprised if you find some cannonballs around or underneath the stern section of the *Heye-P*. Most have concreted into the rock and probably came from the H.M.S. Crocodille, a twenty four gun frigate that went to pieces here in 1784. There are reports that some divers have found a cannon here and that is quite possible because only about fourteen guns were salvaged from the Crocodille. Pieces of pottery, said to be early Ming can also be found in amongst the small gullies or half buried in the sand. This broken procelain might come from the wreck of a Dutch East Indiaman called De Boot, literally The Boat. She was wrecked on *Prawle Point* in 1738 packed with Chinese porcelain stuffed into old tea chests. So far nobody has found a complete piece of this cargo, but who knows, one day it could happen.

With the amount of wreckage available this site is well worth a visit, and not just for the diving, which is pleasant enough, but more for the atmosphere of the whole area. From the shore although the coastline looks fearsome enough, it does not look exceptional. The amount of wrecks however tell the real truth. *Prawle Point* is not really a picnic site. What it really is, is a well disguised ship trap.

Stern section of the
Heye-P

Bow section of the
Heye-P

Above: Bow section of *Louis Yvonne*, stern section of the *Heye-P*

The *Betsy Anna*, one of the lucky ones to escape

CHAPTER 10

THE BOWS OF THE LOUIS SHIED ...
AN EXPERT'S TALE

The *Louis Shied*, well aground on Thurlestone Beach

If you look at a photograph of the *Louis Shied* taken when it was breaking up on Thurlstone beach in 1939, you will see that the bows section points out to sea. Now if you dive on the remains of this once proud ship, you will soon realize that all you are looking at is about three quarters of the ship. There is no bows. All right, that's not exactly gong to disappoint you too much because the *Louis Shied* is an extremely pretty little wreck, and even after all the hundreds of divers that have grovelled over her looking for souvenirs, small brass tallies and valves are still there to be found as the fierce storms continually wash away the sand to reveal other parts of the wreck. I have dived quite a lot on this wreck and have always been rather puzzled as to where the bows might have got to. Once or twice I have made half hearted efforts to find out, but often this has coincided with bad visibility, and in the end I just let the matter drift on unresolved.

Last summer I was concentrating on the shallow wrecks around Hope Cove and found myself snorkelling quite often on the remains of the *Louis Shied* as a last dip before going back to Plymouth. This rekindled my interest in the missing bows, and my friends and I determined to have a serious look for the missing bit the following weekend.

If you do a lot of wreck diving and research, (like I do) it is very easy to begin to think of

the *Louis Shied* splits in two

101

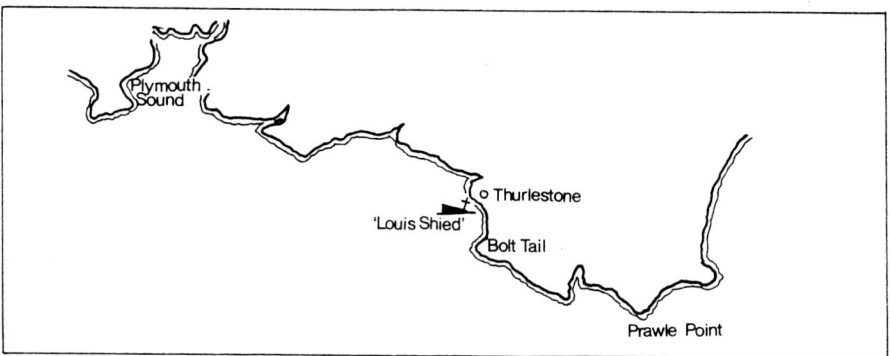

Plymouth Sound

Thurlestone

'Louis Shied'

Bolt Tail

Prawle Point

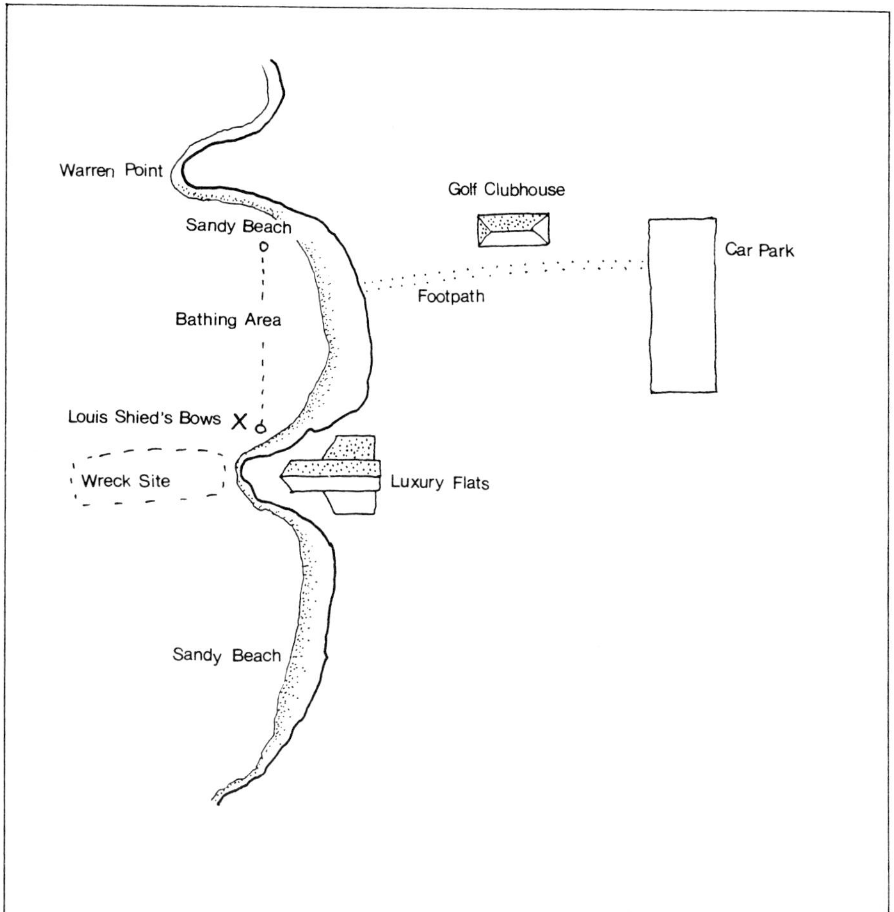

Warren Point

Sandy Beach

Golf Clubhouse

Car Park

Bathing Area

Footpath

Louis Shied's Bows X

Wreck Site

Luxury Flats

Sandy Beach

LOCATION OF THE LOUIS SHIED

yourself as something of an expert. I had studied all my photo's of the *Louis Shied*, written to various people, consulted the coastguard about the possible effects of tide and currents, pottered about the whole area in my boat, and finally convinced myself that there was only one logical place for the bows to be, and that was in the next bay near a rocky promontory. My companions were not so sure. Maybe, they said diffidently, it's a bit closer in, near the shore. Well us 'experts' are nothing if not expert, and I rather smugly gave my partners chapter and verse as to why the bows could not possibly be closer in, and they like the good divers they are, nodded politely and allowed me to get on with it.

That Saturday we did not find anything, but nobody minded because the sun was hot and the sea calm, and it was very nice just swimming aimlessly about. Us 'experts' are used to disappointment but when the next weekend produced much the same result, I could see my grasp of the situation slipping away.

Now it so happened that whilst some of us were swimming about all over the bay, others (getting fed up) had swanned off to dive a bit more on the wreck site proper. It was here, much to their surprise, that they found a large set of bronze thrust blocks crudded into the sea bed. We did not have any tools with us, so reluctantly we had to leave them, suitably hidden under bits of plating. However we decided to retrieve them the next morning, and duly arrived off the *Louis Shied* suitably tooled up. Unfortunately the tide was right out and we could not get the boat near enough to the bit we wanted to dive on, so we decided to anchor up and await the returning tide. Now the bottom hereabouts is all sand with just the odd bit of rock and light anchors are not really suitable. I soon realized we were dragging our anchor and looked about for a better anchorage. As luck would have it there was a rock just breaking the surface right close in near the bathing beach. We'll head for that I thought and stick the anchor on it. The water was really clear, and as I approached the rock I realized that it was much bigger than I had thought, and took care to keep the boat well away whilst my buddy hooked the anchor. As soon as the anchor hit the rock it gave a loud 'clang'. My buddy jammed on his face mask and jumped into the water, surfacing almost immediately with a big grin on his face. Yes, you have guessed it, we had found the bows of the *Louis Shied*.

It was not as big as I had expected, but then quite a lot is buried in the sand. Still there is about fifteen foot sticking out of the sea bed and you can get inside and look out through one of the old hatch openings. The metal is rather jagged however, and there are some nets tangled on it. The whole scene is very picturesque and inside the bows was a small school of bass. There were also quite a few lobsters right down at the bottom, but there is such a tangle of iron plates and netting that it's a bit difficult to get at them. Maybe what we need is another expert.

There is not really much more to tell. I have added a little piece of wreckage to my own private jigsaw, and realize that I still have a lot to learn about wrecks. As to the bronze thrust blocks? Well in the general excitement and namecalling that went on when I 'discovered' the bows we sort of forgot them. As far as I know they are still there.

Inside part of the bow section

The bows of the *Louis Shied*

THE WRECKER'S GUIDE TO SOUTH WEST DEVON

BY PETER MITCHELL

Published by
SOUND DIVING
PUBLICATIONS

Volume 1

THE WRECKER'S GUIDE TO SOUTH WEST DEVON

Now in its second printing The Wreckers Guide Part 1 is a comprehensive guide to how to find all the wrecks under 120 feet from Rame Head to Bolt Tail. Backed up by names and photographs and easy-to-use 'marks' that really put you in wrecksites.

The Wreckers Guide is essential reading for those divers who do not want their day ruined because they cannot find the wreck.

E. J. Rickard LIMITED
PRINTERS OF DISTINCTION
11-13 HOLBORN ST. · CATTEDOWN
PLYMOUTH · PL4 0NN · DEVON
TEL: 0752 660955/662215 · FAX: 266002